Bismarck

BRUCE WALLER

Basil Blackwell

Copyright © Bruce Waller 1985

First published 1985
Reprinted 1986, 1988, 1990

Basil Blackwell Ltd
108 Cowley Road, Oxford OX4 1JF, UK

Basil Blackwell Inc.
3 Cambridge Center
Cambridge, Massachusetts 02142, USA

British Library Cataloguing in Publication Data

A CIP catalogue record for this book is available from the British Library

Library of Congress Cataloging in Publication Data

Waller, Bruce.
 Bismarck.
 Bibliography: p.
 Includes index.
 1. Bismarck, Ott, Fürst von, 1815–1898. 2. Statesmen—Germany—
Biography. 3. Germany—Politics and government—1871–1888.
4. Prussia (Germany)—Politics and governments—1815–1870 I. Title.
DD218.W34 1985 943.08'092'4 [B] 84–28282
ISBN 0–631–13962–1 (pbk.)

Typeset by Cambrian Typesetters, Frimley, Surrey
Printed in Great Britain by Billings & Son Ltd, Worcester

Contents

1 Birth, School and Early Years, 1815–1847

In the spring of 1815, when eleven of Napoleon's hundred days had passed, Otto von Bismarck was born in Schönhausen, a hamlet just east of the Elbe in the Prussian Altmark. Blücher's modern forces and Wellington's traditional army were concentrating for the decisive battle at Waterloo on 18 June which was to end twenty-six years of turmoil. The political and social wreckage of Europe would then be rebuilt by the diplomats assembled in Vienna.

These events, their antecedents and their legacy shaped Bismarck's life and indeed the whole century. The stamp on him was all the deeper because the same forces worked through the agency of his own family. His father, Ferdinand, came from an old and respectable though not especially distinguished family, independent in spirit, yet good servants of their Brandenburg Prussian monarchs. Ferdinand was a typical junker (member of the Prussian nobility) who had rather more of their good than bad qualities. Strong in appearance, easy-going and practical, he was neither educated, pretentious nor unintelligent. Ferdinand was the product of his class and the soil much more than of the time. Yet, unlike his predecessors, he had married beneath his station. His wife, Wilhelmine, came from a bourgeois family. Some of its members had been professors; her father had faithfully served three kings before he died in 1801, and she had excellent connections with the court. Wilhelmine, it is said, was beautiful, educated, intelligent and ambitious; her roots and aspirations were in the town. Thus Otto's parents had different origins, intentions and characters, all of which, inevitably,

1

influenced their son. Historians often point out the clash of parental personalities, attributing this or that trait of Bismarck's to one or the other of them. If one does not ascribe too much to biology pure and simple, there is much to be said for this approach. Bismarck's character was obviously affected by his family background and the different elements in him are traceable throughout his career.

When Otto was one year old, his family moved from the Altmark to Pomerania where none of them were really at home, least of all his mother. In later years, Bismarck often criticized his mother's intellectualism, liberal views and bourgeois pretensions; he also found her much too cold. Throughout his public life he had a tendency to complain, and one must make allowances for this when studying his youth. Still, there can be little doubt that his relationship with his mother was unsatisfactory and that it coloured his life, and, through him, German history as well.

Wilhelmine was not very interested in her offspring as babies or children, but she was extraordinarily concerned about their prospects. She sent Otto to boarding school when he was six, although the gentry as a rule educated their children at home at least until they were a little older. Bismarck was unenthusiastic about the Plamann school he attended, which was probably one of the best then available, but contemporary evidence seems to indicate that he and his classmates were not especially unhappy there. Nevertheless, leaving the countryside for school in Berlin was a trauma. Otto's mother seems to have gone out of her way to prevent visits to his home, Kniephof, among the fields and trees of Pomerania. Perhaps as a result of this, the boy gradually began to identify himself with his father and with his political stance. Throughout his life he was to reiterate his yearning for the country and the forest. These he apparently identified with masculine Prussian traditions and the warmth of the hearth; they represented the instinctive side of his nature. The city became associated with middle-class liberalism, artificial and ambitious intellectualism and, not surprisingly, given his experience, with females. But he did not completely reject his mother. He had her will-power, her ambition and her intellect magnified many times over. And, if we are to believe his memoirs, he had even adopted

2

her liberal, political and religious views when, at the age of seventeen, he emerged from grammar school.

Göttingen was a strange choice of a university for a republican and pantheist – which is how Bismarck described himself in his memoirs. But it was regarded as chic and aristocratic and so, in this respect, was better than Heidelberg. When he arrived he could, of course, have gone to lectures and studied. But, strangely, the young Bismarck was uninterested in anyone but the historian Heeren who was then seventy-two and very much a man of the previous century. Scholars and students in the 1830s were interested in ideals and theory. Heeren was not; he rejected all doctrinaire views, emphasized the significance of material or tangible forces, and advocated moderate constitutionalism along the lines of the French charter of 1814. Bismarck found in Heeren a teacher whose views were similar to those he was in the process of forming himself. One should note the moderate and practical liberalism and the disdain for ideology. His belief in the value of a constitution was never entirely abandoned later on, and his practical approach to politics, later to become *realpolitik*, originates here. In the brilliant old teacher, Heeren, Bismarck found a congenial spirit from whom he could and did learn. But neither in Göttingen, nor later in Berlin, was Bismarck inspired by anything else he saw or heard. He worked hard enough to pass his exams, but most of his time was devoted to social activities. In college he had the choice of joining either the national–liberal and middle-class *burschenschaft*, a fraternity which would have been in line with his intellectual predilections, or an aristocratic club – such as Hanovera – which would be agreeable to his instincts. He chose the latter and in so doing took a fateful step. Most politically active Germans who were maturing then stood in close proximity to the *burschenschaft*. In refusing to tread the familiar path, Bismarck began a lonely political and social climb. He, more than anyone, helped to destroy the *burschenschaft* and the ideals on which it was built. Was the choice in 1832 against the *burschenschaft* and for the noble club a conscious one? The true answer is that it was so only to a very limited degree. His choice was nevertheless instructive. He did not like the manners of the *burschenschaft*. They were earnest and ambitious middle-class

3

town folk, and they did not really interest him. Perhaps he disliked them because none of them fenced (a sign of their lack of breeding). Fencing was one of Bismarck's favourite pastimes; he was in good physical condition and very keen to prove himself. The Freudian significance of fencing for young Bismarck is clear. It is said that he fought twenty-five times in three semesters and won most of the contests. He needed to win these battles and he did.

Bismarck had good looks and manners; he could be witty and clever, so he was a welcome guest in many a salon. But he was unimpressed by society. He was at home neither among the upper classes, whose frivolity he disliked, nor the among the middle classes, whose earnestness repelled him. When he left college he fitted into no obvious slot. He would have to make one of his own, and at this stage it seemed as if he would not succeed.

After university, Bismarck tried his luck in the civil service. In Prussia an arduous and uninspiring period of practical preparation was needed. This he did at first in Berlin and later in Aachen, then a renouned spa, whose temptations the young Bismarck found harder to resist than office routine. Aachen was popular with the English. Bismarck had taken some trouble to learn their tongue in addition to French. The history and culture of Britain he had long found almost as attractive as his own German traditions. Now a new dimension was added: English girls, Miss Russell (a niece of the Duke of Cleveland), and his first real love, the unusually beautiful Isabella Loraine-Smith. She so turned his head that he abandoned work without bothering to obtain leave – so he lost his money as well as the job. For months he followed her around Germany like a puppet on a thread. He thought they were engaged to be married late in 1837, but she jilted him for, as he erroneously claimed, an elderly but wealthy one-armed colonel.

After this fiasco Bismarck made a weak attempt to return to office work, this time in Potsdam. There followed almost a year of national service, during which time, on 1 January 1839, his mother died. Shortly before this, Bismarck left the civil service, explaining the reasons for this decision in what we might call his first confessional letter to his cousin (*Die Gesammelten Werke*, xiv, no. 27). It boiled down to one characteristic argument: the Prussian official is like an individual in an orchestra, but Bismarck wanted to make the music he liked or none at all. However, he recorded his doubts as to whether he would be up to such a task. A further comment is also instructive: that constitutional states were preferable to absolutist Prussia – he would like to be someone like Peel, O'Connell or Mirabeau. The letter clearly reveals the unresolved tension between the three strands of his personality, his will to power, his intellectual liberalism and also his conservative, rural instincts – he concludes that he had better retire to the country where he would seek fulfilment.

He had hardly arrived home when he began to kick over the traces. Of wine and women he took what he could get; he played practical jokes on his friends and fully earned the epithet of 'wild Bismarck'. He fell in love again and this time was properly engaged, but the lady's mother would have nothing to do with him. He even had another try at the civil service, but the job lasted a mere two weeks. This was the less productive side of his existence which led nowhere. While he sowed wild oats, he also cultivated proper ones. He read widely about social problems and history as well as some modern literature. He travelled and so extended his horizons. In addition, he made his estate pay for the first time. He learned something about the continual ebb and flow of nature and began to see what effect it had on him as well.

These were experiences which could be sensibly utilized, but they were not, until he met Marie von Thadden in 1842. Then his life changed rapidly. The adolescent became a man. His years in the wilderness were over. Marie was the fiancée of Bismarck's close friend, Moritz von Blanckenburg. She, her family and her circle of friends were pietists, that is Lutherans with a simple faith in God. They by-passed Church hierarchy by preaching the gospel to one another; theirs was an uncomplicated and undogmatic faith based on feeling and brotherly love rather than intellect. Church attendance, and indeed the whole formal side of religion, did not matter to them. It was also not unimportant that several of the pietists, especially the Gerlach brothers, were close to the romantic Frederick William IV who had just become king in 1840. Through the pietists the sinner was brought back into polite society and introduced to some of its most distinguished – if cranky – members. Bismarck began talking about religion with Marie. Their attraction for one another was immediate and electric. She had never met anyone whose views were so outlandish and convincingly argued. He was impressed by her piety and intelligence.

How she was able to win him over will forever remain a mystery. If anyone could, she was well qualified, and the time was ripe as well. Bismarck could see that his previous life without ethical direction had led nowhere. And her type of religion offered a great deal to a man like him. It allowed him alone to decide what his relationship to his Lord should be; he would not be merely a musician in an orchestra.

Marie took it on herself to save a soul and was aided by her friend Johanna von Puttkamer. Together they worked on Bismarck and achieved what few others could; they converted him. Although there are some unconvincing aspects in his conversion, most historians agree that it was genuine. Henceforth he prayed and read the Bible off and on, but he carefully followed the daily maxims and verses of the Moravian brethren year in and year out. There were, as he once said, hidden folds to his soul behind which no one could peer. What actually clinched the conversion was Marie's sudden and untimely death in an epidemic. Faced with this calamity he prayed for the first time in fifteen years. Within weeks he proposed to Johanna, Marie's religious accomplice. To win her he had to write his brilliant second confessional letter, this time to her father (*G.W.*, xiv, no. 71). The tone is confident and cold but it is also brutally frank as far as his own many failings are concerned.

Historians cannot agree as to the extent of the changes wrought by Bismarck's conversion. It did not make him into what we may call a Christian statesman, but it did give his character sufficient direction and integration to enable him to play an effective role in public life. His career began immediately and his rise was meteoric.

Johanna was in many ways a replacement for his mother, who had died eight years before their marriage. His father had died in

1845. In a poetic mood he once wrote about 'a home filled with love, a quiet haven into which a wind from the ocean storms might occasionally blow, rippling the surface, but the warm depths of which remain clear and peaceful, so long as the Lord's cross reflects in it' (*G.W.*, xiv, no. 184). For the first time he had unquestioning backing from a woman. Because of this, his views on the world and women softened somewhat, but he remained hostile to assertive and intellectual females. His religious feelings gave him sufficient moderation and sense of responsibility to lessen the tension existing between his trenchancy, his instinctive conservatism and intellectual liberalism. For the first time, Bismarck's personality possessed an element of harmony.

2 *Realpolitik*

From the time of Luther to the end of the Thirty Years war in 1648 with the Peace of Westphalia, the clash of religious conceptions seemed to guide the conflict between states. Then, in the period from Westphalia to the start of the French Revolution in 1789, the more tangible considerations of state consolidation and growth were clearly paramount; religion or ideas mattered less. This was the classical age of *raison d'état*, which was followed by a period during which the role of ideas was again primary. First the revolutionary theory, then the countervailing conservative idea dominated European politics until 1848. More often than not, political disputes were influenced and even decided by ideological considerations. Most politicians were willing to sacrifice material welfare to the tenets of one or other ideological creed.

Realpolitik (realistic politics) must be understood as a reaction to this state of affairs. It was an attempt to break the iron bands of ideology. If we were to set other-worldly idealism and personal activism (adventurism) at opposite ends of the political spectrum, the next position towards the centre would be occupied respectively by ideological and power politics. *Realpolitik* would be somewhere in the middle. If these terms are to have meaning, we must be careful not to confuse *realpolitik* with *machtpolitik* (power politics). The difficulty in definition lies in the fact that the only pure forms are the two extreme positions. The three in the middle are, and have to be, unstable mixtures of aims and means from all the positions on the political spectrum. The lines dividing them are feathered and each approach incorporates aspects of the others. One must not expect *realpolitik* to be something radically different from ideologically governed policy. The latter would

8

even share some, although much less, common ground with *machtpolitik*. If we contrast Bismarck with the liberals of his day, as indeed we might, we should guard ourselves from the temptation to view the motives of the one as of this world, and those of the others as originating in a higher and more ethereal sphere.

The word *realpolitik* was coined by Rochau, a disappointed national-liberal idealist of sorts who felt that the tragedy of 1848 stemmed from an excess of idealism, and that more practicality or realism would be needed with reference both to goals and means. *Realpolitik* was not at the outset conceived as the opposite of idealism, but rather as idealism with a sufficient amount of power awareness to be viable.

Bearing in mind the origin of the word, it could be said that *realpolitik* was merely a more modern version of eighteenth-century *raison d'état*. Before the storming of the Bastille, *raison d'état*, or state oriented policy, was calculating and amoral to a degree, mellowed only by the personal whims of the prince. *Realpolitik* also focused on the interests of the state, but among these interests the ideological element was present although not prominent. It took the place formerly occupied by princely caprice. Since the First World War, however, the situation has been reversed yet again: ideological considerations are now weightier. Because the role of ideas in the Middle Ages and most of modern History was critical, Bismarck's Europe seems to have been a somewhat untypical period, in some ways worthy of the nostalgic feelings we have for it. But the hard-headed selfishness of the age shared by liberals and others is less attractive.

The discrepancy between Bismarck's views and actions before and during 1848 and those after 1862 is so startling that historians, not unnaturally, have sought to explain it with reference to his long educational process in Frankfurt, St Petersburg and Paris; and there is much to be said for this explanation. In his recent biography, however, Gall argues for a much more rapid development of Bismarck's views, which he believes were worked out in principle before he went to Frankfurt in 1851. For Gall, Bismarck's place on the political spectrum was closer to *machtpolitik* than to *realpolitik* throughout his life. He has not uncovered new material to support his views, but he does make extraordinarily good use of already well-known evidence, as we shall see.

When Bismarck found a wife and a home, he also discovered religion and self-knowledge. His life changed overnight. An active interest in politics was awoken during his conversion. The arduous process of the emancipation of the serfs in Prussia had been started at the beginning of the century by the great reformer Stein. At the same time manorial justice was curtailed. During the 1840s there was much discussion as to the future of its remnants. Showing remarkable lack of foresight, Bismarck backed the more conservative suggestions advanced by friends of the ladies who were converting him. Apart from deputizing for a local official, his first responsible act in politics was the acceptance of the office of dyke reeve. In 1845 the Elbe had badly flooded Schönhausen – the estate still owned by his family – and the ancient lime trees, standing sentinels around the house, were uprooted. Bismarck blamed this on the incompetence of the local reeve whom he was determined to displace. The position was minor, but it did have a certain symbolic significance for his future career; and it was also of vital importance locally and so helped to introduce him to the surrounding gentry, some of whom, surely, were surprised by this evidence of public spirit. Through these connections he managed to become elected as a substitute member (the first in the queue) of the provincial diet. This meant that when the United Provincial Diet met in Berlin, and one member could not attend, he went in his place for the last seven weeks of its session. After the defeat of Napoleon, Frederick William III had promised his people a parliament, but could only bring himself in 1823 to grant separate provincial diets with little scope. To obtain financial authorization for the construction of a railway a joint meeting of the several diets was convoked for the first time in 1847 and they began sitting in April.

While a student, Bismarck is reported to have said: 'a constitution is unavoidable and the way to formal honours, but one must first be sufficiently pious (1901, ii, p. 246). And it was indeed through this Diet, and its efforts to obtain a constitution of sorts, that Bismarck first attracted attention. One can, of course, see microscopic signs of his subsequently realistic approach to politics in 1847, but we must not magnify them. His activity was largely based on instinct and fired by his own volatile personality. The view that he was at this time embarrassingly and idiosyncratically conservative is justified. Rather than evidence of *realpolitik* we see eloquence, irascibility, unfairness and the instinct of a hunter. All this was used in defence of the aristocracy against all comers and the monarchy against most. Bismarck was not completely absorbed in politics yet, and dashed off on an extended honeymoon immediately after the dissolution of the Diet in June 1847.

After the outbreak of revolution in March 1848 the United Provincial Diet was recalled and sat in April. Bismarck participated in its deliberations, but for the rest of 1848 he watched the game while running up and down on the sidelines. He helped to found, and wrote articles for, a newspaper known as the *Kreuzzeitung* (so-called because an iron cross was emblazoned on the title page). He also participated in a landowners' protest meeting in August 1848, rather grandly titled the Junker Parliament.

On the surface, Bismarck's position does not seem to have changed much from the previous year; nevertheless, as early as 2 April 1848 we see what could be an example of exasperation, or perhaps the beginning of a trend towards constitutionalism and a more practical approach to politics. On that day he suggested in the Diet that the new, revolutionary ministry in Prussia might make order out of chaos because the past had been buried and the crown itself had tossed soil on its own coffin (*G.W.*, x). A good reactionary would not have said that, and his political associates did not appreciate it either. In the summer he used the pages of the *Kreuzzeitung* and the podium of the Junker Parliament to speak more clearly: he accused his opponents of crass materialism, but nevertheless recommended it to his friends. He also tried to mobilize public opinion for the conservative cause. We can see here that the instinctive and pugnacious conservative was beginning to come to terms with the modern trend away from bureaucratic monarchy towards constitutional and public politics. (One might mention that in those days German liberals wanted

11

merely this, nothing more. The demand for parliamentary government was radical and advanced by few.) Bismarck surely knew that conservative ends could well be pursued but never attained using the methods he proposed. He still spoke out strongly against liberalism and nationalism, but was at the same time letting some of their attitudes in by the back door.

Bismarck was a member of neither the German nor the Prussian national assembly in 1848, although he stood for the latter. When in the autumn the revolutionary tide was ebbing fast in Prussia as well as throughout Europe, Frederick William dissolved the Prussian assembly and decreed a moderately liberal constitution. Elections for a new assembly took place immediately; Bismarck received a mandate and so entered the public arena. By this time the Frankfurt National Assembly had worked out a bill of rights and a constitution for a liberal and united Germany to be led by an emperor who was to be a visible link between the past and the future. The dignity was offered to Frederick William who refused what he termed a 'crown of clay': that is, he did not relish a title resting on the approval of the crowd rather than his peers or the traditional divine right. The Prussian king was not in principle disinclined to take the lead, however, and so tried to talk the German princes into offering more or less what the Frankfurt Parliament had done.

On 6 September 1849, during debates in the Prussian lower house on this matter, Bismarck delivered the first truly 'Bismarckian' speech. Its contents typically bore little relation to the ostensible purpose. Here was an orator pleading for a Frederician policy: after the rejection of the imperial title offered by Frankfurt, Prussia could have either joined Austria and decisively defeated the revolution, or disregarded Austria and dictated her own constitution to Germany – come what may. But disaster could only result from the king's attempt to compromise with revolution: Prussia would be doomed if unification should be achieved with the consent of the other princes. In other words, one could be for or against the revolution and the national-liberal cause, but whichever path was chosen, one should march down it to the sound of Prussian trumpets (*G.W.*, x). Bismarck ostensibly argued the case for the conservative right and against the king's scheme for unification. But this speech shows that, whatever he was, he did not appear to be conservative. Nor did he seem to be a liberal; he was certainly bellicose. What contemporaries found disturbing and chilling was his tendency to see in black and white (the Prussian colours), and his reluctance to assume a less firm, but perhaps wiser, stance.

His position is more clearly shown in another speech, delivered immediately before his appointment as Prussian representative to the revived German Bund. Frederick William IV had continued to pursue his own project for German unification until he was forced by Russia and Austria at Olmütz in November 1850 to make a humiliating retreat. The Bund which had been abandoned in 1848 was revived and Prussia, to her disadvantage, forced to join.

When the unpopular Olmütz agreement was announced in parliament, on 3 December 1850, Bismarck had the task of defending it. Whether he was really for or against the agreement is uncertain. He had celebrated the events leading up to it by riding around his table astride a chair with a glass of sparkling wine. But a fortnight before the speech, he had advocated an extreme anti-Austrian line. The way he accomplished the task of defending Olmütz is interesting and warrants further attention.

Bismarck argued that when considering the question of peace or war, politicians must base their policy on the interests of society as a whole: a statesman must justify war with arguments which are valid afterwards as well as beforehand. What he meant was that the dispute between Prussia and Austria was not worth a war. Although the speech was apparently pro-Austrian, he did in fact hint that, should the Hapsburgs not grant parity within the Bund to his king, war might well be justified. To win such a conflict, however, Prussia would need to co-operate with the revolutionaries, and this, Bismarck argued, was inadmissible: 'The only sound foundation of a great state – and therein lies the essential difference from a small state – is state egoism and not romanticism; and it is unworthy of a great state to fight for something in which it has no interest' (G.W., x). The remark about romanticism referred to ideologies on the right as well as on the left. What he would have regarded as Prussian interests then

13

it is not easy to state, but the definition would certainly include more than economic considerations. Having said this, the stark realism of the rhetoric is impressive: only those who are weak can afford Quixotic humanitarianism; the strong are obliged to grab what they can.

Bismarck had entered politics with views on the idealistic side of *realpolitik*. By the end of 1850, on the eve of his appointment to Frankfurt, his views were on the power political side of the mean. He had reached this point relatively quickly; subsequent evolution back in the direction of idealism was slow.

The public defence of the 'humiliation of Olmütz' won Bismarck the appointment of envoy to the confederation, an important job not usually reserved for beginners. This gave him eleven years to learn the trade of diplomacy and helped to shape his views on politics in general and foreign policy in particular.

Until the end of the decade there was little apparent change in Bismarck's approach, although he elaborated his views in long-winded reports. In letters and despatches he argued persuasively that politics is not a science with quantifiable or even hidden rules in need of professorial exegesis, but the art of the possible, and that it should be concerned with the retention and extension of power and not the defence of principle. He reiterated time and again that foreign policy, especially, should be based on a hard-headed appreciation of one's own country's interests: 'sympathies and antipathies concerning foreign powers and individuals I cannot justify to my own sense of duty in the foreign service of my country . . . therein lies the embryo of disloyalty to the master or the country one serves' (*G.W.*, xiv, no. 647). What is disturbing is that some of the things he suggested do not on the surface fit that purpose. His own combative personality, rather than the art of the possible, comes through strongly in the advice given on the eve of the Franco-Austrian war in 1859: 'If we allow Austria's war against France to grind on we can have the "lucky draw" and march southward with our whole army, taking the boundary markers in our rucksacks and driving them in again on Lake Constance or wherever the Protestant faith ceases to predominate' (*G.W.*, xiv, no. 724). Whether joining the French and starting a civil war could have succeeded then is very doubtful, and this shows that not everything written on the banner of *realpolitik* was realistic. Where here is Bismarck's proverbial sense of timing, and where is the caution he so often advised – or the two irons in the fire? When it came to specific issues, Bismarck did not aways heed his own invaluable general advice. His policy was frequently very risky and we must be careful not to call luck statesman-ship.

The contours of Bismarck's version of *realpolitik* emerge perhaps most clearly in an almost hundred page report written in March 1858, known as his booklet (*G.W.*, ii. no. 343). He had previously advocated co-operation with France to stop Austria, and no one had listened. Such a policy might have helped to increase the might of the Prussian state, but it was also probably neither in the interests of the German people nor the Prussian establishment – that is, it was revolutionary without being national or liberal. Now Bismarck looked for support from German public opinion, the national-liberal movement, advocat-ing more freedom for parliament and the press. The argument that there was nothing more German than the pursuit of properly understood Prussian interests amounted to the recognition of the validity of the popular movement which he had ridiculed in the past. This was a development of critical importance. By approaching the national-liberal movement, Bismarck began to absorb the kind of idealism which, combined with toughness, could give his policy direction and effectiveness. The previous policy of pure state egoism could not suffice. To gain the needed support, it had to be associated, however tenuously, with a loftier ideal.

By the end of the 1850s, the details of Bismarck's *realpolitik* were fully visible. Its driving force was furnished by his bellicose character and this explains his lack of dogmatism and consistency, which he often referred to with pride. He put it most succinctly perhaps when he said that having to go through life with principles is like walking down a narrow forest path with a long pole in one's mouth (Poschinger, 1895–9, ii, pp. 166–78). As we have seen, he did have principles, but not those that were widely shared by contemporaries, and he was imaginative in his interpretation of them. The initially very strong instinctive conservatism was somewhat weakened by the hardening of still relatively weak constitutional and national convictions.

His conception of *realpolitik* was rough and ready, and he acted accordingly wherever he could get away with it. A study of his justly famous politial writings in the 1850s illustrates this. But when he took office in September 1862, his actions showed that he was capable of moderation and good sense where these were absolutely necessary. Still, we must admit that prior to this date there is little to indicate that he could be relied on to know when to stop – indeed hardly anyone thought he did. After 1866 the moderate character of his political approach gradually strengthened – not without many fits and starts – to such an extent that the Bismarck of the 1850s would certainly have reproached the Bismarck of the late 1880s for lack of courage and energy.

If we return now to the point of departure for this brief discussion, it looks very much as if Bismarck's approach to politics had indeed undergone considerable and rapid change until his appointment as envoy in Frankfurt. But a later, and in some ways more important, process of mellowing took quite some time. Gall is very nearly right in his assessment of Bismarck's development, but he does tend to dwell rather too much on the power political strand of Bismarck's foreign policy. The German historian, Treitschke, once wrote that the essence of the state is first power, second power and third again power. This was probably Bismarck's view at the beginning of the 1850s, but at the end of the decade he had moved perceptibly away from it. He never, however, went so far as to pursue an ideal which conflicted with interest of the state.

In the period before his appointment to the cabinet in 1862, we have ample evidence as to Bismarck's general views on politics; we also know what course of action he proposed during the crises of the preceding decade. These policy statements shed little light, however, on his tactical approach. His ability to size up allies and opponents, to make use of their foibles, as well as his willingness to change stride with a cavalier's disregard for consistency, are visible. Versatility in action is not. His sense of timing looks conspicuously poor. No doubt he learned these things on the battlefield and not at the writing desk. Excellent as were

Bismarck's judgement and timing in office, he made many mistakes throughout his career; fortunately for him, others made more.

The frequently expressed and sincerely meant religious humility acted as a brake on his tempestuous temperament. It did not make a saint of a sinner, but it did keep his sins within bounds. And more than this, his faith gave him the conviction that whatever he personally wanted was also God's will. It was not only easy, it was also right to stand up to opposition. In 1851, mixing conceit with piety, he wrote: 'God lightens my burden, and with Him I am more effective than most of our politicians who could be in Frankfurt instead of me and without Him' (*G.W.*, xiv, no. 322). His own words express as well as any the role of religion in his politics: it was an obstacle to extreme action, yet it strengthened his resolve in most matters.

Bismarck's writings until his appointment as prime minister reveal the rapid maturing of an acute, pessimistic, practical and cynical mind. They were not recorded to provide material for scholars but rather to persuade colleagues and kings. In fact, the two kings, Frederick William IV and William I, probably never even read his longer efforts, and the other recipients were not amused. Bismarck's writings, like many of his actions, were counterproductive.

Bismarck was not appointed to high office because he had a profound, albeit rather materialistic, understanding of Prussian interests; he was appointed rather because he promised to do the king's will – like a good Brandenburg vassal – when his master was in danger. It should not have been difficult for the inner circle to anticipate the line Bismarck would follow, once entrusted with the state seals, but their lack of comprehension was nearly total and hardly improved with time.

3 Bismarck and German Unification

Bismarck's view of politics was essentially that of a realist, and his approach to domestic and foreign policy imaginative, energetic and practical. In this chapter we shall look at his foreign policy; the next will deal with his views on nationalism and the idea of a constitution.

We have seen that Bismarck's first faltering moves in politics were in the domestic sphere. But well before his appointment as envoy to Frankfurt in 1851 his concern was mainly with foreign policy. What he knew about the functioning of politics he learned from a study of foreign affairs. His handling of Prussian and later imperial business betrays this in unmistakable ways.

Traditionally politics in Europe has largely been concerned with foreign affairs – the dealings with other princes and other states. Such things were regarded as, and in fact actually were, more important than domestic policy – as long as a revolution could be avoided. With the advent of the industrial and democratic revolutions all this began to change – slowly at first, but by Bismarck's time with increasing rapidity. The historian Ranke emphasized the primacy of foreign policy, especially in central Europe. In the 1960s, however, a school of German historians began to insist that the reverse was true, that domestic policy was dominant. With reference to the twentieth century this view is plausible, but the further back we go, the more dubious it is. Still, one thing has emerged: in Bismarck's day domestic and foreign affairs conditioned one another. Exclusive concentration on foreign affairs can only yield part of the truth.

In his memoirs, Bismarck insinuates that from the start he had worked for the unification of Germany. There is other evidence to reinforce this contention: for instance the remarks he is supposed to have made on a visit to London during the summer of 1862, when at a dinner party he spelled out to Disraeli more or less what subsequently happened. He said that when he was in charge he would initiate the reform of the army, find a pretext for war with Austria and destroy the Bund. Unfortunately, since the source of this is neither reliable nor contemporary, it is open to question – quite apart from its own inherent improbability. But, if it is true, it illustrates his energy, acid frankness and intention to try his luck with the national-liberal movement in 1862. The further back we go through the previous decade, the harder it is to find any contemporary source showing Germany's George Washington at work – quite the reverse. If Bismarck did not have everything mapped out in advance, is the opposite version more likely? Did he follow a purely day-to-day policy, as A. J. P. Taylor would have us believe?

By way of illustration let us look at three points Taylor makes in his biography of Bismarck (1955). He suggests that before 1866 Bismarck did not intend to disrupt the existing order in Europe unless events drove him to it. After victory over Austria in that year he had no vision of future action. The war with France in 1870 took him by surprise and was most unwelcome. In other words the fabled lion was in fact a lamb; Bismarck's contemporaries and generations of statesmen and scholars have been wrong about him. This reading is unlikely since it offers no other explanation for Bismarck's ascendancy than the notion that he followed a lucky star. Bismarck was indeed lucky, but this does not in itself explain his achievements. We must think of an explanation which will allow for a considerable amount of planning and foresight, but also for flexibility, irrationality and downright opportunism as well. We have seen how his approach to politics evolved. How did the policy itself change?

It is not without significance that some of Bismarck's earliest statements on foreign policy differ from the view expressed in his memoirs. On 21 April 1849 he said that though all those who spoke the German tongue wanted unity, he scoffed at the idea that Prussia should follow the example of Piedmont in Italy

(*G.W.*, x). Later on he continued to refer to Piedmont's folly in joining forces with the revolution. At this time, of course, Piedmont's policy of expansion was singularly unworthy of emulation. Within ten years the situation was different.

In April 1849 Bismarck seemed to be a supporter of Austria. By September, the first doubts appeared when he said that Frederick William could either co-operate with Austria or perhaps go against her, depending on the needs of Prussia. Here, when the Hungarian revolutionaries had been finally defeated, we have the origin of Bismarck's deepening animosity towards Austria. The two alternative policies were again eloquently expressed in the *Kreuzzeitung* in November 1850, where he demanded parity with Austria, and then in his great Olmütz speech on 3 December in which he preached state egoism. This must have meant to anyone with a well-tuned ear that solidarity with Austria had no especially high priority. Yet the speech must have been almost universally misunderstood. The conservatives duplicated it by the thousands and distributed it throughout the country, although from their point of view it was really quite subversive. Ironically, the speech won for Bismarck the appointment as Prussian envoy to the Frankfurt Diet – where he was expected to co-operate as much as possible with Austria in the interests of conservative solidarity.

A few years later Bismarck claimed: 'I was certainly no opponent of Austria on principle when I came here . . . but I would have had to deny every drop of Prussian blood, if I had wanted to retain even a moderate preference for Austria as she is conceived by her present rulers' (G.W., ii, no. 23). When Bismarck arrived in Frankfurt he may not have been a determined opponent of Austria, but he was also far from being a friend. He was in fact resolved to take as much as he had to give. The trouble was that Austrian policy had evolved considerably since 1848. Before this, Metternich had tried to run the German confederation along Austrian lines but without estranging Prussia. Indeed, the Prussians had been treated almost as equals and they in turn were good allies. But after Austria had struggled for survival and for her place in Germany during the revolution of 1848 as well in the aftermath, though really a weakened state, she continued to fight vigorously for an undeserved position of pre-eminence. In the conditions of the time Bismarck's demand for parity would have involved only a slight improvement over the earlier set-up. So in comparison with Austrian pretensions his initial aims were moderate and tenable.

We have already seen that while in Frankfurt Bismarck's political approach changed very little. But he rapidly became disenchanted with Austria and his animosity grew. His initial belief in the feasibility of either a pro-Austrian or an anti-Austrian policy (without allies) faded, and he had to seek support elsewhere for the conflict he foresaw. Much of his thought in the 1850s was devoted to the search for appropriate support at home and abroad. It may well be wrong to argue, as many historians do, that Bismarck strove to climb the heights between two camps so as to be able to descend in one direction or the other. In fact his views became gradually more decisive.

It would have been accepted practice for Bismarck to start off in Frankfurt following a policy gentle in manner and firm in purpose, but his manners were abrasive and petty from the start. This publicized his cause, though it cost him sympathy and complicated his task. In the circumstances, the judgement of the Austrian envoy Prokesch probably represented the general view: Bismarck could occasionally behave as a gentleman but had an arrogant, common and pompous nature; he was lazy and lacked a sense of justice as well as sound knowledge and a respect for it; he was adept at sophistry and the use of trivial and unclean methods; for Austria he showed envy and hatred which explained his battle against her rights as head of the confederation; he was an atheist but had Protestantism inscribed on his battle flag (Wertheimer, 1930, p. 34). This was the opinion of an experienced and scholarly, though not altogether tactful, diplomat – not an excitable novice. Bismarck's relations with his likeable prede-cessor, Thun, or his irritable successor, Rechberg, were no better.

The blend of personal and political animosity that appears here is a thread which weaves its way through Bismarck's politics throughout his life. In this case the personal and political enemy was one and the same, so the feuds intensified the growing political difficulties with Austria but did not cause them.

Trouble started first on the economic front, with the Prussian policy of developing the *zollverein*, which was established in 1834. Before this all the German states had had their own customs arrangements. But they gradually abandoned them and joined Prussia in one free trading area (the *zollverein*, or customs union). The Austrians were to be kept out. In stark contrast to the co-operative political line generally followed in this decade, Prussia remained firm and Bismarck applauded. By this time both Prussians and Austrians were aware that the customs union might well have an explosive significance. Austria's difficulty was simply that the material interests of most German states bound them to her relatively more free-trading rival. The young Prussian envoy neither made nor influenced his country's trade policy since trade negotiations were conducted in the two capital cities. But he quickly saw how they could serve his own purpose, for by the end of the first year at his post he was convinced that the clash of Prussian and Austrian interests would, and probably should, eventually lead to a division of Germany into a Protestant north and a Catholic south. This profoundly anti-national goal, then dimly perceived, was unattainable with the weak tool of the *zollverein*. The obstacles were many. Austria's strength was still appreciable; as the former head of the Holy Roman Empire she was also the representative of imperial tradition and the promise of a German future. Neither Prussia nor her leaders were capable of a struggle; nor could allies easily be found. Bismarck needed luck and he got it. He had to exploit the errors of others, and he did. He needed to refine strategy and tactics; here he succeeded as well. He also tried to impose his wisdom on colleagues and superiors; in this, however, success eluded him for years, and the influence he gained was never assured.

The Crimean War gave Bismarck his first important opening. During the war both Russia and the Western powers looked for allies, or at least support from whatever quarter they could find it. For obvious geographical, political and military reasons the position of Austria was critical. She was caught between the two opponents, had a poor hand and played it badly. Russian favour was lost, but none was won in the west. To the south the Italians became restive; to the north the Germans were disheartened.

Still, her own pretensions remained unaltered. Cavour, the prime minister of Piedmont, was the first to reap a harvest from the changed situation. But Bismarck was the first to seed his crop. Right from the start of the war he saw the possibility of benefiting from Austrian embarrassment. Bismarck's line became harder and more clearly defined. On 26 April 1856, what is known as his 'splendid report' (*G.W.*, ii, no. 152) spoke of the inevitability of an armed trial of strength emerging from Austrian – rather than Prussian – pretensions. Since both were ploughing the same disputed field, Prussia therefore should seek French as well as Russian support. Although there were diplomats in St Petersburg and Paris who could easily imagine such a combination, there were, apparently, none in Berlin.

The 'splendid report' shows two things. War with Austria would be hard to avoid: henceforth Bismarck could not rid himself of this idea. As Austria's position in foreign affairs continued to deteriorate he saw less reason to avoid war. The report also shows his understanding of Prussia's need for some kind of outside help. In 1856 she would have needed substantial help (but not so much as Piedmont); a decade later, appreciably less. Russia was an obvious source of aid; but France continued to be the embodiment of revolution. To obtain support from this quarter he would necessarily have to abandon conservative ideology and perhaps accept territorial loss too. This would be difficult enough; and since German liberals also had strong national feelings, it would be virtually impossible to gain their co-operation so long as Prussia fought for limited goals, because a moderate expansion of Prussian power would destroy the Bund and therefore weaken German unity. In April 1856 Bismarck said the struggle would be for Prussian existence, but even if it were a struggle for the division of Germany into two spheres of influence it would make little difference. Once Bismarck sought help from revolutionary elements, he would have to yield something to both liberalism and nationalism. Although his goal in the mid-1850s appeared modest – an even split with Austria in Germany for a conservative Prussia – from this point a dynamic element was introduced. By 1866 a row between cabinets for limited objectives had gradually become a struggle for supremacy in Germany to be won in co-operation with the revolutionary forces of liberalism and nationalism.

It is possible to exaggerate the singlemindedness of Bismarck or Cavour. We can see that Bismarck's policy concerning Austria, that is, concerning Germany, was developing before 1856. After the 'splendid report' the picture is very much more clear. That he began steering a collision course cannot be denied, nor can the probability that his initially limited goal would become more ambitious. Indeed by early 1858 he was arguing that Prussia should look to the German national movement for support. This was new. A year later he said, as he logically had to, that Austria must be removed from Germany proper.

The events of spring 1859 – the defeat of Austria by France and Piedmont – turned an idea into a distinct possibility. Prussia was still weak, but on the mend; Austria was by this time equally weak and slipping fast. The Italian example inspired Germans and Prussians alike. A national association was founded on the Italian model and looked to its Piedmont – Prussia. Some kind of alliance, however tenuous, with Russia and France was clearly feasible. And so therefore were Bismarck's ideas, especially when in his Baden-Baden memorial of 1861 (*G.W.*, iii, no. 234) he proposed a patently Piedmontese line, leaning even more heavily on the national and liberal component than hitherto. Bismarck knew that Prussia on her own was still too weak to challenge Austria and achieve even limited goals, such as parity with Austria or an equal division of Germany between the two. But, with popular help within Germany and some foreign connivance, he believed she could attain much more. The problem was that no one listened. The king, the conservatives and the liberals all regarded him as an adventurer. William, who became king in 1861, had been deputizing for his incapacitated brother since late in 1857. As soon as he was made regent a year later, he replaced his brother's conservative ministers with mildly liberal men whose views were in some respects much nearer those of Bismarck. Although the new ministers were not fond of the quarrelsome envoy in Frankfurt, they dared only promote him to out-of-the-way St Petersburg in 1859, where he was very unhappy but learned much from the Russian foreign minister, Prince

Gorchakov, who was then in his prime and whose approach to politics was a more sophisticated version of his own.

To his great relief, in 1862 Bismarck was accredited in Paris which he visited on his way to Biarritz for a holiday, whence he was called to Berlin in September 1862.

During the Franco-Austrian war in 1859 the Prussian army was mobilized. Things went so badly that not only the officers, but also the public felt that the army was in the same pitiful state as before the ignominious defeat by Napoleon in 1806. We can illustrate this by quoting passages from *The Times* (1 and 6 November 1860) which yield an interesting comparison of English and Prussian prowess. Rather arrogantly, the London paper wrote:

> We can fight our battles, whether it be necessary to defend our own shores or to send 100,000 men to the other side of the earth to reconquer an insurgent province. Prussia unaided could not keep the Rhine or the Vistula for a month from her ambitious neighbours . . . Prussia is . . . always getting somebody to help her, never willing to help herself . . . . She has a large army, but notoriously one in no condition for fighting.

We may take it that the need for a general reform was widely recognized. The snag was that William and his minister of war, Roon, wanted a royal army; the liberals – and many others – wanted a popular army. The ensuing bitter quarrel was not about whether the army should be reformed and expanded but how this should be done. Neither side was prepared to give way. William wanted to make a last attempt to force acceptance of his views before capitulation, so he summoned Bismarck. Neither William nor Roon had previously fully understood Bismarck's numerous reports or accepted his views. In 1862 he was made prime minister and given the portfolio for foreign affairs because he was thought to be tough – which he was – and conservative – which he was not. Both the king and Bismarck were gambling. So far Bismarck had been extraordinarily lucky. Many things had gone in his favour with little effort on his part. In future he would have

25

to make his own way and earn his luck. The army reform was doubly significant. If parliament rejected it he would certainly lose his job and Prussia would probably be unable to risk war with Austria. These two considerations – the personal and the political – go a long way towards an explanation of Bismarck's tempestuous behaviour during his first months in office. His public reference to 'iron and blood' on 30 September 1862 (*G.W.*, x) just a week after his appointment to high office was inopportune, but a perfect reflection of his political views and state of mind. The speech, by the way, was not war-like and Bismarck's conduct was reported in the press as 'conciliatory'. Although Bismarck's comment referred mainly to the need for the army reform, the purpose for which 'iron and blood' were to be used he made crystal clear to the Austrian envoy in December. He expected the Habsburg empire to move to the south and east, leaving Germany for Prussia. On Christmas day he told the king how this was to be done: by replacing the confederation with a democratically reformed *zollverein* (*G.W.*, iv, no. 18). This simple formula meant a great deal: the exclusion of Austria was to be achieved with the co-operation of the national movement and the political and economic sides of the liberal movement. An expanded Prussia would have to be less conservative and provincial and more German and liberal. Bismarck's problem was to supervise this revolutionary change without losing office.

Since the customs union treaties were up for renewal during 1865, the critical point would then be reached. It was necessary to be ready. Although it is true that Bismarck would probably have accepted a peaceful solution which granted him the substance of his demand, it would be untrue to argue that he worked for anything but a military showdown. His activity at home and abroad really allows for no other interpretation. Its twists and turns should not be allowed to confuse us and one wonders whether they were indeed necessary or even useful.

Bismarck's real achievement at home was obtaining the money for the reformed army. This allowed him to remain in office. By hinting at good things to come he crippled the national liberal opposition, but in the process he lost the backing of the conservatives. Abroad he capitalized on the avarice, stupidity, indifference or connivance of the major powers. Their mutual rivalries made his task very much easier than he and his admirers would have us believe.

British policy was one of amicable indifference. Despite Bismarck's masterful line at home and abroad, London remained more suspicious of other powers throughout. Russia was closer to home and had borne a grudge against Austria since the Crimean war. Bismarck's support during the Polish uprising in 1863 was embarrassingly zealous, but did, on balance, lead to improved relations. France was pacified through the hints of gains in territory and prestige. A business deal à la Cavour bought Italian troops: Italy was promised, and subsequently got, Venetia. The reaction of these powers was neither surprising nor difficult to anticipate. Unless one assumes an inevitable series of blunders, Austrian policy was less explicable. The political and social make-up of the country did not allow Austria to toy with nationalism and liberalism. She did so all the same out of fear that, if she did not play and win the game, Prussia would. The policy was nothing short of disastrous. The attempt to check Prussia by a joint adventure in her rival's own northern sphere was misconceived from the start. Francis Joseph's role in the Austro-Prussian war against Denmark in 1864 was in some ways similar to Louis Napoleon's part in the 1859 war against Austria. A national war could only lead to a temporary gain in Austrian popularity in Germany. The division of the spoils with Prussia arranged in 1865 at Gastein made Austria look egotistical and foolish – egotistical because a national war had led to a virtual Austrian annexation. Foolish because Holstein, Austria's share of the booty, was too close to Berlin and too far from Vienna for comfort. In some respects Prussia's position seemed equally bad, having taken Schleswig in the bargain, but at least Prussia was very largely German (Austria was mostly non-German), her policy of expansion looked 'national', her record of economic liberalism was good, and her promise of political reform appeared marginally more sincere.

The die was finally cast in February 1866, when almost simultaneously the Austrian emperor decided to defend his over-extended lines and the Prussian king made up his mind to attack

27

them. What was more, he also agreed to join up with the revolutionary forces of nationalism and liberalism in Germany and beyond her frontiers. Bismarck had finally brought him round to this. At the battle of Königgrätz (1866) the Prussian soldiers fought for a modern Germany; the Austrian troops battled for an aging empire.

That many Prussians instinctively felt this to be the case is shown by the results of the elections on 3 July, the day of Königgrätz. For the first time there was a clear swing towards Bismarck and away from the opposition. The voters knew nothing of Prussia's victory; in fact many must have believed she was marching into the abyss. This might well have been the time for a massive vote of no-confidence. But the Prussian electorate rallied around the flag and indulged in an exercise of wishful thinking; in addition, they were beginning to change their minds about their arrogant and masterful leader.

The unexpectedly rapid and complete Prussian victory decisively affected Prussia and Germany as well as the position of both in Europe. The establishment of the North German Confederation and the initiation of a decade of reform turned Prussia into a more liberal and more national state. Neither Bismarck nor the national-liberal movement hoodwinked the other. They drew closer to one another and they did so willingly. The lenient treatment of Austria dulled the inevitable desire for revenge and facilitated the healing of painfully deep wounds. After the war, Bismarck had to contend with mounting French and diminishing Austrian animosity, rather than, as might be expected, the reverse. French standing in Europe was based on a weak or a paralysed Germany. Napoleon had hoped that Austria and Prussia would bleed one another white and that he could deal with the convalescents at his leisure. Clearly, the strengthened Germany that emerged was unwelcome; a yet more consolidated Germany could, in addition, be dangerous. It would not necessarily be a threat, but it could easily be. Napoleon desired therefore at least to stop further German unification, or even better, to weaken the existing set-up by obtaining compensation from Germany or elsewhere for her apparently weakened international position. At best he could teach the Prussians a lesson by reducing their territory or sphere of influence. What should be noted is that whereas the Austro-Prussian clash had an air of fatality about it, the necessity for a war between the North German Confederation and France was much less. The former led to a quick reconciliation; the latter to enduring enmity.

France and Austria shared a common wish to weaken the Prussians. But the differences between them were far greater. That this was so is testified by the fact that both could live with the results of 1866. First their secular rivalry hindered co-operation: neither Austria nor France wanted the other to prosper too much. There was also a clash of interests in the Balkans and elsewhere. But most of all the two countries differed in their attitudes towards German nationalism. France had to oppose it; this Austria could never do. For Austria neither victory nor defeat in a war with Prussia was desirable because either would destroy the internal balance achieved in 1867 between the German Austrians and the Hungarians. A year after defeat at the hands of Prussia, the Habsburg monarchy was split into two nearly independent states. The eastern part was run by the Hungarians, the west by the Germans. Since in each part Slavs made up half the population but had little say, the balance was delicate. The Hungarians were especially interested in maintaining this 'compromise', that is, they did not want to see the German element either weakened or strengthened. The German Austrians did not want to fight fellow Germans on behalf of the French because even victory would bring trouble. Since the French believed they could beat Prussia and her satellites unaided, there was no apparent need to secure allies with whom they would have to divide the spoils. In those days the French regarded themselves as the world's best soldiers; Prussians and Germans in general were thought of as ineffectual and comical.

After Königgrätz Bismarck began to think that war with France might not be so easy to avoid. He felt that in certain circumstances it might even be useful. Napoleon was less astute, less vigorous and less single-minded, but his attitude was virtually the same, that is, he felt that war was probable and perhaps no bad thing.

The Luxemburg crisis in 1867 was a gift to Bismarck. The area was German-speaking; it had belonged to the Bund and was still a member of the *zollverein*. Napoleon's clumsy attempt to take it could easily have been used as a pretext for a popular war. And such a war could further the cause both of Prussian aggrandizement and German unification. But it came too soon. The North German Confederation had hardly got off the ground. It was also advisable as a demonstration of his willingness for stability to let a good opportunity for war slip by in the interest of peace.

The opening provided early in 1870 for a member of the Hohenzollern family to mount the Spanish throne was, on the face of it, far less promising. Although the new north German state was not yet consolidated, it was at least established. Links with south Germany had been strengthened, but a tendency for the south to go its own way was beginning to emerge. Perhaps it was time to act. It would be foolish to argue that Bismarck wanted to avoid war and the fortunate results war could bring; he did not aim at a diplomatic triumph. His sights were set high. He had little respect for the statesmanlike qualities of Napoleon or the French nation, and probably believed that the two, working on one another, would produce a cancerous growth of foolishness. Indeed his policy depended on this. With luck he would have war, for which Moltke (chief of the General Staff) was prepared; if he had neither good luck nor bad, something at least, would certainly come his way. The purpose of secret negotiations for the candidature was to produce an electrifying shock when they finally became known. The candidacy was treated as a private family matter to ensure increased frustration in France and added indignation in Germany when the reaction came. What Bismarck did not anticipate was a loss of nerve on the German side. When the crisis reached its height in July 1870, and the French reacted with anticipated intemperance, William agreed to withdraw his candidate. Bismarck cannot have been happy. Had the French accepted this in good grace as a resounding and easy diplomatic victory, he might well have had to negotiate a redundancy payment. But they played right into his hands and asked William to promise that the candidacy would never again be revived. Like Austria in the spring of 1866, France in the summer of 1870 anticipated victory and captured regimental standards; she felt no need to accept a diplomatic trophy.

Both Bismarck and Napoleon were prepared to accept modest gains, but both preferred the prize that only war could offer. Napoleon fought for traditional French ascendancy in Europe; just as Francis Joseph's justification in 1866 was historical, so too was his. By contrast, Bismarck fought to make Prussia a modern and German state; for justification he looked to the future. The Franco-Prussian war resulted in a victory for Germany in 1871; Bismarck was made a prince and chancellor of the new German empire.

4 Bismarck, the Nation and the Constitution

As a youth Bismarck was exposed to the conservatism and provincialism of his country surroundings, personified by his father. Urban and liberal views filtered through to him through his mother. The marks of the pull of such contradictory forces on an intelligent but volatile nature can be seen throughout his whole career. Conservatism seemed to dominate in 1848. Afterwards he slowly began to see the usefulness of liberalism and its related force, nationalism. Although liberalism and nationalism are barely reconcilable social concepts, they nearly always went hand in glove in nineteenth-century Europe. Bismarck drew nearer to liberals and nationalists, adopted some of their ideas, but without much real conviction. In this section we shall look at Bismarck's relationship first to nationalism and then to liberalism as reflected in the Prussian and imperial constitutions.

Nationalism

Bismarck was neither a German nor a Prussian nationalist in the customary meaning of the term. And it would be pointless to tailor a definition that would suit him but few others. Hans Rothfels was probably close to the truth when he argued back in the 1930s that Bismarck's thought focused on the historically evolving state rather than the nation, that is the institution rather than the people, although he did, as we have seen, adopt some of the programme of the nationalists. From this perspective the popular dispute about the point at which German nationalism emerges from the Prussian cocoon becomes senseless. An

32

approach like Bismarck's in the Germany of that day is not surprising. Who could say what Germany was? Views differed widely. The German principalities, however, were realities. The state also took priority over king and class as far as Bismarck was concerned, although he was devoted more to these than to the nation. This emerges clearly in the Schleswig–Holstein dispute where it is likely that he would have preferred to see the Germans remain there with the Danish crown if Prussia could not get them. Nationalism of whatever political hue is coloured heavily with emotionalism and we can see traces of this in some of the things Bismarck said. There are many expressions of derision and contempt. Some of the worst refer to Poles. For instance: 'Strike the Poles so that they despair for their lives. I have every sympathy for their plight, but if we want to survive we cannot but exterminate them' (*G.W.*, xiv, no. 815). There are also compliments of sorts for Prussians and Germans along conventional lines. He referred to his own people's honesty, industry, orderliness, dependability, correctness, frugality, simplicity, and so on. But we do not see pronounced racial prejudice. (The word 'race' was used more loosely then than now.) However, if we are honest, we can cite disdainful remarks about all manner of people and things. A tabulation of the flattering and unflattering things he said about his own people – or his own class – would surely show a heavy preponderance on the negative side: Germans, he thought, were petty, impractical, self-righteous; the gentry had neither intelligence, manners nor horizon. So although there is a trace of romantic attachment to his earth and his people, Bismarck's devotion to the state was more potent and was largely a matter of the mind. He could subtract from or add to it at will. Disraeli was right in thinking that Prussia was no nation. It was at most a collection of provinces animated by a state ethos and a dedication to the ruling house.

Before Bismarck assumed high office he realized that in order to survive, Prussia would have to modernize, that is, abandon some of her conservatism and provincialism. He was determined to facilitate this change in such a way as to remain in control. He did so with calculation – not enthusiasm. In the past, Prussian leaders had not been especially mindful of a German mission.

Polish land and subjects were also dear to them. There was nothing automatic about the expansion of Prussian power in Germany. But for an accident of history, Warsaw would have been Prussian and not Russian. One could argue that Prussia was programmed more by her history to evolve in the direction of a dual monarchy than to become the centre of a German empire. Bismarck himself said as much, but he chose the second option because he recognised that more substantial and permanent gains could be made by working together with a popular movement. He gradually came round to this view; but the probability remains that, had Austria tried to buy off Prussia by dividing Germany between them, Bismarck would have been sorely tempted almost right down to the outbreak of war in 1866.

Calculation tightly reined Bismarck's weak national sentiments. The more German Prussia became after 1866, the more the Poles had to take a back seat. They had been loyal Prussians, but they were less willing to become Germans than their German-speaking brethren. This is, however, exactly what they were expected to become. The pressure to conform became steadily heavier; but the results were meagre. When in power Bismarck backed these attempts not because he wanted to turn Poles into Germans, but because he felt that so long as they remained essentially Catholic Poles their loyalty to the state would be minimal. Had he worn only his German national coat he would not have encouraged the heir apparent in 1870 to teach Polish to his son, later to become William II, claiming that he knew the language himself. And he repeatedly said flattering things about the Polish peasant. The clergy and nobility, he thought, were the misguided souls. During his term of office much was done for the Poles – particularly in education. On the other hand, although Bismarck did not go as far as the national extremists, he did authorize some rough treatment.

For the Polish people it made little difference that his carrot and stick approach was rational rather than enthusiastic. The acrimonious debate amongst contemporaries and historians as to whether the Poles were trouble-makers or victims has not been fruitful. And the search for guilt at this level is misguided. In the west there was, and is, a reasonably clear geographical separation

34

between French and German speakers. In the east the nations were thoroughly mixed, so that in a period of almost universally growing nationalism trouble was unavoidable. The demonic force of nationalism is illustrated by the fact that although by 1914 Catholics, Jews and workers felt more at home in Germany, the dislike of Poles and Prussians for one another was deteriorating to hatred. Bismarck's idiosyncratic but calculating approach had limited scope and probably added just a shade of sanity to an otherwise morbidly insane conflict. Whether in the circumstances more could have been achieved is doubtful.

The same rational attitude towards the national movement can be seen if we examine Bismarck's motives for backing the annexation of Alsace and part of Lorraine. Later on in life Bismarck was strangely silent on what could be regarded as a great national achievement. The little he says in his memoirs looks apologetic. Historians have long believed that he was pushed into annexation by the military and a powerful movement of public opinion. This is clearly wrong: right from the start of the war in July 1870 he was in tune with public opinion in demanding annexation; he even encouraged the cry for the lost German provinces.

Haller was about as near the truth as we will ever get when he wrote in 1917 that Bismarck 'spurred on the galloping horse' of public opinion. The military, however, was curiously silent on annexation until the matter had been decided by the beginning of September. Bismarck's motives were traditional rather than national. He wanted to get something out of the war, especially a more defensible frontier since he believed the French would seek revenge with or without Alsace and Lorraine. In 1888 he bluntly told the viceroy in the provinces that Alsace-Lorraine was not annexed out of consideration for its inhabitants, but rather to reinforce the German border with France (Rogge, letter on 14 May). This utterance is a fair reflection of his attitude towards the newly-won compatriots across the Rhine. There was also a tactical motive: the demand for annexation prolonged the war and gave him time to complete the negotiations for establishing the empire. The German character of the provinces meant something to him, but not much. Perhaps this was because he knew that although they spoke his tongue, their hearts were French. It is not surprising that the German majority in the new provinces was treated relatively well, but it is worth noting that the tiny French minority received better treatment than the Poles. This may have been partly because they were few, but backed by a proud and powerful nation. Bismarck made this point graphically when in 1871 he apologetically spoke to the French of the danger arising from the annexation: the two provinces were an embarrassment – a Poland with France behind it (*Documents*, i, no. 42). The important point is that Bismarck's line on both the German- and French-speaking citizens here was determined mainly by their degree of willingness to co-operate with the empire. A heavy hand was used frequently in the Polish part of Prussia, but less often in Alsace and Lorraine. The French minority had a great deal more cultural autonomy than did the Poles.

These two case studies, as it were, illustrate Bismarck's cool approach to nationalism. It can also be seen in his reluctance to extend the imperial frontiers to include more Germans. Those beyond the pale in 1871 had to remain there. For him there was no *Germania irredenta*. Nevertheless, the Pan-German League first idolized and then selected him for honorary membership. Here we see not only human craftiness or historical irony, but, probably even more, understandable confusion.

Constitution

Bismarck's conception of the place of a constitution and a parliament in political life was limited. His ideal state was the Prussia of Frederick II, or the ancestors of the Great Elector; that is, it was monarchical or aristocratic, according to his mood. But this was a dream world, not the real one, in which a constitution was useful. Properly worded, a constitution would of course limit Bismarck's own power, but, more importantly, it would also limit the power of countervailing forces – the king, the bureaucracy, the army and his opponents in politics.

The Prussian constitution was not in any way Bismarck's doing. He condemned both universal suffrage and the three-class electoral system, advocating instead the representation of occupational groups. Later on, especially in the 1880s, he returned to the idea. Still, he learned much from the way the constitution functioned. First of all, he saw how an originally liberal instrument could be amended or twisted to change its spirit, he realised that in certain circumstances parts of it could simply be ignored. He also saw how, if the various elements are balanced, whoever is at the fulcrum can push things one way or the other at will, and large weights can easily be shifted. A skilful man at the centre could wield a disproportionate amount of power. As early as 1851 he likened the constitution to an empty vessel whose contents are determined by those in power (*G.W.*, i, no. 36). The constitution decreed in December 1848 provided for a two-house legislature: the lower house was elected by universal suffrage, while the upper house also had an elected element. Such an arrangement made at such a time was entirely understandable, but given the conservative structure of society then, and the ebb of the revolutionary wave, it was not workable. Subsequent changes made the upper house into a House of Lords, but one much more dependent on royal influence than its model in Britain. For the lower house the three-class electoral system was introduced which gave vastly greater weight to the votes of the wealthy. This, together with indirect and publicly cast votes, was supposed to insure stability. It did so for a few years, but towards the end of the 1850s it merely led to the pre-eminence of the wealthy – a plutocracy, with the townsfolk leading the gentry, not the other way around. Had things worked out as planned, the landed classes would have dominated, unchallenged. Bismarck could see that for his purpose – and incidentally for the good of Prussia too – the unintended balance eventually created by the reformed Prussian constitution was workable. When it led to a deadlock whoever was at the centre could apply the 'gap' theory, play off one side against the other and have his own way. In the Prussian constitution the king and parliament were supposed to legislate jointly; there was no provision for deciding what to do in case of a deadlock. There was a 'gap' in the constitution which was visible right from the start. Bismarck and others believed that the government could act on its own until the conflict had been resolved. As we know, the dispute over the army reform led to such a deadlock and during the course of the dispute Bismarck made full use of the 'gap' theory. Taxes were collected and money disbursed to pay for the army reform without reference to parliament. He did not, however, push for a total triumph. After the victory over Austria in 1866 he asked parliament to 'indemnify' his action. This amounted to an implicit recognition of parliamentary rights and was all that the more realistic of Bismarck's opponents had worked for before the war. The constitutional dispute ended therefore in a compromise. Bismarck believed that a constitution with a liberal colouring would appear to be modern and so help to ensure support from the educated public. If it were, in addition, 'anointed with a drop of democratic oil', it would appear progressive as well, and tie the common man to him. Bismarck was convinced that the healthy peasant or man in the city street was conservative and could be used as a counterweight against the aspirations of the liberal middle classes. He was also convinced that his own luminous intelligence would contrast favourably with the strong but angled light emanating from the parties. Unfortunately, his own mind did not glow as steadily as he thought.

Bismarck's experience with the Prussian constitution taught him that he had little to fear from nationalists, liberals or those farther to the left. Yielding in even fairly important issues would not necessarily diminish his personal position of power or lead to cataclysmic change. This attitude was put into practice in the few months after Königgrätz – perhaps the most productive of his career. During this time he came to terms with the Prussian parliament, produced a reasonably liberal constitution for the North German Confederation, and won over much of the opposition – although in doing so he lost the support of most of the conservatives. Bismarck put this fertile combination of imagination and restraint into classic form when he wrote: 'a statesman can only listen for the Lord's footfall echoing through events, then have the resolve and presence of mind to leap forward and grasp the hem of his garment' (Meyer, 1933, p. 7).

The constitution of the confederation established in 1867 – which became that of the new German empire set up in 1871 as well tried to reconcile three irreconcilable aims, and its achievement in this respect is probably more remarkable than its failure. It was designed to preserve strong government and as much of traditional society as possible. It adopted as many liberal reforms in politics and the economy as appeared to be beneficial. It had a democratic element too – universal and equal manhood suffrage and the secret ballot – to harass the middle-class liberals apparently from the left, but, Bismarck hoped, actually from the right. The federal structure with its profusion of parliamentary and other institutions put into practice a further balancing act. Prussian dominance was to be secured, but just barely enough to suffice in crucial matters and not so much as to offend the theoretical sovereignty of the other princes. Prussian provincialism and that of the other states would also be curtailed in the process.

The north German constitution provided a parliament with two houses. The lower house was elected by universal suffrage. The upper house consisted of representatives from the governments of the member states. Parliamentary procedures were quickly adopted. In its first decade, parliament established the imperial institutions on a reasonably liberal footing. Despite what legions of students and, unfortunately, some historians believe, the German empire had a constitutional government which was quite capable of enacting laws in tune with the spirit of the age. What imperial Germany did not have was parliamentary government. The parliament had very extensive powers but it lacked one which was crucial. It was not so important that there was only one responsible minister – the chancellor. It did matter, however, that he was not responsible to parliament, but rather to the upper chamber and the emperor. To be enacted, laws had to receive his approval and that of both houses of parliament as well. A certain amount of political chicanery was therefore needed if the system was to function – and it did function. Of course Bismarck and his successors had the upper hand and they used it occasionally, but not as frequently as a casual observer would think.

If it is wrong to say that imperial Germany was without constitutional government, it is absurd to argue that her government was absolute, or even semi-absolute. Certain comparisons may be made with the Napoleonic style; the strong, even wilful government; the adventurous foreign policy during the first eight years, and the unsteadiness afterwards; and the liberal and democratic forms which seemed to mask something more insidious. But there are also essential differences: the emperor, not Bismarck, held ultimate power; the strength of parliament was considerable; freedom of speech and freedom of the press were marked; the law was sensible and respected. Bismarck was the author rather than the heir of revolution. And, reckless as he surely was at times, he had more than a Napoleonic degree of moderation.

The word 'Bonapartism' is not really helpful in assessing Bismarck's style of government. His mixture of old and new ideas on domestic and foreign policy was unique. He was not a typical junker, even a clever junker, who manipulated nationalism, liberalism, democracy and socialism. He yielded too much to these 'isms' for that. He was also not simply a leftover from cabinet diplomacy, or the opposite: a characteristic figure of his age. The phrases 'red reactionary' and 'white revolutionary' may point to the problems, but they miss the nuances. In short, he is a subject for historians and not so much for sociologists, as Böhme and Wehler would have us believe.

5 Imperial Foreign Policy

The ceremony on 18 January 1871 in Versailles marked a watershed of national achievement for Germany, and personal achievement for Bismarck. No other event during his term of office had comparable symbolic force. So many Germans had worked and prayed for the creation of a powerful and modern nation-state. This they now had, and everything was changed. Yet, the more closely one examines the period, the less distinct the break becomes. Attitudes, in particular, lagged behind events. Bismarck's foreign and domestic policy was changing, but not as rapidly as it would seem. Certainly, eight years of disruption (1862–70) were followed by nineteen years of moderation (1871–90). But he who had been relatively moderate in war was to be restive in peace. So although we must take the great event in the Hall of Mirrors at something less than face value, it still remains a turning point dividing Bismarck's public career into two. But each of the four decades also has its own character. The 1850s and 1870s were periods of transition leading, the one to the active 1860s, and the other to the inactive 1880s.

Historians have long debated the question of the extent of the German victory of 1871 and its significance in European history. We should not lose sight of two things. First, although Europe and the world were changing rapidly in 1870, we must not attribute all these changes to the results of the Franco-Prussian war which were more modest than is sometimes assumed. The other point to keep in mind is that the German empire was not at the outset very much stronger than France. Germany's population was slightly larger and her army was very much better. But she was less united than France and her economy was more

41

precarious. Intelligent contemporary observers had a right to believe that France would soon recover. Although it was, of course, possible to see that Germany would slowly pull ahead of France, those who did believe this were few and their numbers did not rapidly increase. To put it another way: German hegemony evolved after 1871; it was not created by victory in war. All the powers were uneasy about the extent of Bismarck's victory. This was partly because it altered the balance of power and indirectly led to the establishment of what many regarded as a greater threat to the social and political peace – a French republic. Diplomatists also wondered where Bismarck would turn after this, and who would be his next victim. They were not sure whether it would be Holland or Austria. Of the great powers, however, only France felt threatened by Germany, and they all (including France) tried to come to terms with the new empire. The result of this was that by the end of 1874 Berlin had become the centre of an informal group. Had fear of German hegemony been widespread this would have been inconceivable. Austria and Russia were bound by a written – though empty – agreement, the Three Emperors' League. Italy was openly friendly, while Britain was more distant. But France was without allies. She had reluctantly, albeit faithfully, submitted to the German conditions of peace; the government had, as well, shown as much goodwill as circumstances allowed.

One thing had changed in Europe and that was to become painfully clear to Bismarck during the 'war-in-sight' crisis of 1875. All the foreign ministries naturally wanted good relations with the German empire, but none were amenable to a further extension of German power. Prussia had been apparently unworthy of their attention; the empire was not.

Prussians and Germans had gained victory, an empire, two provinces and five billion French francs, yet at home old quarrels revived and new ones appeared. The economy was badly shaken by the onset, in 1873, of a depression which was to linger until well past Bismarck's departure from office, and its impress on German society, and perhaps on men's minds, was to be more permanent than the influence of Bismarck. France, on the other hand, seemed to prosper through adversity. A broad recovery was in full swing; the army was improving fast. Bismarck hoped that co-ordinated German; sabre-rattling would impede that recovery. This is what was behind the 1875 war scare, but the result was entirely counter-productive. France received firm diplomatic support from England and Russia and weak assistance from Italy. Austria stood aside, trying to look neutral, but hoping that Germany would be taught a lesson. In May 1875 Berlin was isolated; a few months earlier it had been Paris which had stood alone. The significance of the incident did not escape Bismarck. Hitherto he had endeavoured to tip the balance of power in his favour, thus enabling him to keep the French in place. Afterwards, his approach became more devious and dynamic. He sought security less through a favourable balance of power than through what Medlicott calls a 'balance of tension'. This was a change in tactics and strategy, but not of goals. Of all the numerous memoranda setting out his political views, perhaps the clearest expression of this approach can be found in the memorable Kissingen dictation of 15 June 1877. The Russo-Turkish war was barely underway and the French Government had just carried out a potentially dangerous coup d'état on 16 May. The situation was precarious. Bismarck thought that the ideal solution from a German point of view would not be any kind of territorial gain, but rather a political constellation in which all the powers, except France, needed Germany and were kept from forming an opposing coalition through their relations with one another. He illustrated this idea with reference to Anglo-Russian relations: it was in the German interest to encourage links between England and Russia which could produce mutual relations as good as at the beginning of the century and promise the friendship of both with Germany. An eventual agreement granting Egypt to England and the Black Sea to Russia, would keep both satisfied with the status quo for a long time, although their vital interests would keep them in rivalry and also well away from participation in anti-German coalitions (*Grosse Politik*, no. 294).

We have here Bismarck's own account of his approach to foreign affairs from the 'war-in-sight' crisis until his retirement. With little exaggeration it could also be taken as the epitome of his policy from 1871 onwards. And with hardly more exaggeration we can regard it as a distillation of the whole of his foreign and domestic policy. The approach is pessimistic yet active, and any interpretation of Bismarck's policy in peace time must take account of this. We can see strands of continuity with the period before 1870. The approach was pessimistic because it made no attempt to overcome tension, merely to guide it. He felt that man's combative nature was like bad weather; one could take shelter but could not prevent it. Gladstone hoped to humanize international politics through co-operation. Bismarck felt such attempts were Utopian or even harmful because those who had no keen sense for the realities of power could easily get themselves and others into serious trouble. His policy was also active because he relied on the continual balancing of tension. Constant vigilance and effort, employing 'fair means or foul' were needed. The means were varied and much too imaginative to be appropriately characterized by the word 'system' which implies a more static approach. Two and a half years after the Kissingen memorandum, Bismarck told the Russian ambassador, Saburov, that all politics could be reduced to the formula: to try to be one of three so long as the world is governed by the unstable equilibrium of five great powers. This maxim is frequently cited as illustrating the core of Bismarck's foreign policy. While its practicality, freedom from moral judgement and mobile readiness are typical of the man, it is not quintessentially Bismarckian. He wanted rather to be the nucleus of European politics than one of a gang of three (Simpson, 1929, p. 111).

The best study of the two decades of international relations after unification is still Langer's superb book, *European Alliances and Alignments* (1931). His views were strongly coloured by the effort to take a fair-minded view of imperial German foreign policy after the excesses of the propaganda of the First World War. According to Langer, Bismarck was the chess grand master who dominated the board not in the interests of war but of peace. His work for peace was tireless and effective – which is more than can be said of his contemporaries in office who, through carelessness or intent, inclined repeatedly towards war. To change the metaphor, Bismarck was not only the architect of peace, he was also its custodian. Langer's prose becomes rather fanciful when he writes with reference to the crisis of 1887: 'had he not been there, the nations would have had it out in the good old way. They had often fought on less pretext. But for Germany's sake, Bismarck desired to avoid any conflict in Europe' (Langer, 1931, p. 453). Far from condemning tension, Bismarck created and preserved it in order to channel it into ostensibly less harmful colonial disputes. Langer regards this as a policy based on reality. He defends even the last three years of Bismarck's diplomacy, which on the surface seem unnecessarily devious and futile. This image of Bismarck canonized has dominated the historical scene for the past fifty years, but, as we shall see, it has major faults.

First, the magnification of Bismarck's importance does not alter the facts. Bismarck overshadowed, but did not obscure, his friends and rivals who neither needed nor appreciated advice, threats or coaxing. Second, Langer and his readers idolized peace. Bismarck did not. After 1871 he sought to avoid war for practical reasons: the circumstances were not opportune. Had they been favourable, perhaps he would have taken up arms again. He feared a general conflagration because the consequences were incalculable, but he did not oppose limited war between two European powers. He must in fact bear some of the responsibility for the only European war waged in the period 1871–90, that between Russia and Turkey in 1877. He encouraged it, hoping that a little blood-letting would make the Russians more amenable. His policy here illustrates his belief that countries spoiling for a fight should be turned away from Germany rather than stopped. One might also stand Langer on his head as Marx did Hegel. Perhaps Bismarck's actions would have led to war had it not been for the good sense of the other European statesmen. In 1874–5 his belligerence nearly provoked conflict; and at the end of the 1880s his tricky manoeuvres could easily have misfired. Even Langer must suspect this, otherwise he could not write that when Bismarck left the stage it was more difficult to maintain the peace. His image of Bismarck as the architect and custodian of the peace is but a charcoal sketch. He has the main lines of a flattering likeness with reasonable accuracy. But we need more detail and colour.

45

In assessing Bismarck's statesmanship, we must not forget the unfortunate influence of his personal shortcomings: his emotional nature, excitability and vindictiveness. His nerves were bad; they had never been especially good and years of struggle had frayed them further. His great intellect was usually (but not always) a sufficient check, and his hatred of real or imagined enemies occasionally blinded him. He persecuted opponents and ridiculed uncongenial ideas. Towards the end of the 1870s, the increasingly intense campaign against Gorchakov, Russian chancellor since 1867, is a classic example of this. By 1879 it had reached the magnitude of a personal cold war. The two chancellors fought ostensibly for their own country's ascendancy amongst the conservative powers; in fact they strove increasingly for personal triumph. Bismarck won; Gorchakov's career was snuffed out like a candle; and their countries' relations received a jolt at the moment they began to deteriorate, partly because of the diminishing success of economic co-operation, but mainly because of the political friction produced by the rapid rise of Prussian power and pretensions, and Russia's reluctance to accept a relative decline.

Historians have always recognised the adverse effects of Bismarck's vindictiveness on domestic policy, but they have been strangely reluctant to see them in his foreign policy. However, looking at the results of the 'two chancellors' war', we see how important the personal factor could be. Since Gorchakov was a very old man and was at the end of his political tether, the futility of Bismarck's vendetta is especially striking.

Implicit in Langer's view of Bismarck's statesmanship is the claim that Bismarck had a plan ready for every eventuality. This is questionable. By contrast, A. J. P. Taylor has argued that Bismarck 'lived in the moment and responded to its challenge' (Taylor, 1955, p. 33). Medlicott, however, is surely closer to the truth in his view that Bismarck's approach was a combination of long-range planning and tactics.

The chancellor's excessive trust in his superior tactical ability mounted with the passing of time. He owed his skill in tactics partly to a profound pessimism. He did not believe in the propriety of advance payment for goods to be received later:

politics was largely a series of specific bargains. Convinced that this approach made good sense, he did not worry much about the long-term consequences of his diplomacy. His freedom of manoeuvre was therefore extraordinarily great. The trouble was that the other participants did not play according to his rules. None were prepared to sacrifice vital interests on the altar of idealism, although most were willing to suffer small losses. They resented Germany's reluctance to co-operate with others unless something was offered in return, and they were upset by Bismarck's cynical disapproval of their real or pretended high-mindedness. In the Balkan troubles in the 1870s and the 1880s, for instance, the Russians felt that their line was sincerely Christian; the British were convinced that their opposing view was humanitarian. Bismarck believed neither. But in attempting to convince each that he was on their side he repeatedly manoeuvred himself out of one difficulty and into another.

The way the *kulturkampf* was waged involved Germany in both unforeseen domestic and external troubles. The same could be said for the manufacture of crises to obtain parliamentary approval for the army bills. The dual alliance with Austria in 1879 may well have been concluded for largely tactical reasons although it was to become the keystone of a structure of alliances; it probably created almost as much trouble as it overcame. And during the last three years in office, the alliance network looks more like patchwork: one agreement after another mended weak spots with pieces of different cloth.

Historians are reluctant to see anything but genius in these manoeuvres but one should ask whether more straightforward methods might have proved more suitable, or even if the moves were made very skilfully. Many German historians, even some of those most critical of Bismarck, have argued that a Goliath was needed to protect their country. But is it not a plain truth that the protection of a satisfied and powerful empire was as easy as the expansion of a weak Prussia was arduous? Prussia might have needed genius at the helm; the empire needed merely steady nerves and common sense for the preservation of the status quo. Conceivably, the other powers could run rings around a stationary Germany, but the likelihood of this was virtually non-

47

existant. The opposite result would have been much more probable: a steady empire would have benefited from the rivalry of others.

Bismarck may not have been so interested in the preservation of the status quo created in 1871 as Langer would have us believe. Alternatively, perhaps his view of what the preservation of the existing order involved needs analysing. Bismarck repeatedly stated that the German empire was satiated. Apart from the fact that a man of his acumen and record would naturally say this to avoid shock waves reverberating through Europe and back onto Germany, if we consider for a moment that another war might lead either to disaster or the glorification of the generals and army at his expense, and that a worthwhile prize was nowhere in sight, we can take Bismarck's statement at face value, at least as far as it concerned the territorial shape of the empire in Europe. We do know, however, that in the 1880s he succeeded in establishing an overseas empire, so that Germany's satiety clearly did not apply here. But even looking at international relations within Europe, Bismarck surely wanted a position of ascendancy which was neither traditional nor guaranteed by the Treaty of Frankfurt of 1871. He, the author of turmoil and revolution, tried to unite the conservative powers against France and to play the dominant role in this grouping. Here we see the dynamic element in Bismarck's foreign policy. And his effort to be always in the midst of things explains to some extent the activity and changes in German foreign policy which were otherwise unnecessary. The policy of territorial expansion during the 1860s had been sublimated, as it were, transported onto the diplomatic plane. His trophy, the German Empire, had been won with a struggle; he could not understand that it could be protected in any other way. This led him to seek security through an inventive and continuously active policy guided by instinct, rather than by a compass.

Most historians regard 'the Bismarck system' as merely the network of alliances and alignments which were tied together by Bismarck to preserve peace and German security. Fearing enemy coalitions, he carefully made one of his own. On the face of it the change in Bismarck's political approach is astonishing. Before the

Franco-Prussian war he was the great destroyer of systems. Afterwards, his approach looks conservative and institutional, and is not unlike that of Metternich.

The traditional view is that Bismarck began devising his 'system' during the Franco-Prussian war, or shortly afterwards, and that the plans were gradually extended, so that the system became more extensive and also more rigid. Following this line we can distinguish three phases. The first began in 1873 with the Three Emperors' League, with which Italy became associated because of her concern about the dangers of militant French Catholicism. Through this informal alliance Bismarck sought to achieve two goals: to isolate France and to restrain Austria and Russia. He hoped the league would allow him to keep an eye on both his partners. Thus he could prevent them from allying against him or coming to blows with one another and dragging him into the fray. Unfortunately for Bismarck, the Balkan crisis from 1875 to 1878 nearly shattered the whole thing. Austro-Russian antagonism was acute, each country fearing that the other would make disproportionate gains; and not only was Bismarck almost drawn into a war, but the Russians wrongly felt he had sided too strongly with Austria. So after the Congress of Berlin in 1878 which attempted a Balkan settlement, a more substantial structure was needed for the original purpose, but it also had to control Russian aggression. The core of the second phase of the system was therefore a defensive treaty with Austria, the dual alliance of 1879, aimed against Russia. On top of this, the Three Emperors' League was renewed in 1881. Of course Russia's position within it had taken a blow. In 1882 Austria and Germany allied with Italy as well against France and Russia. Then, a year later, Romania added her support to the increasingly anti-Russian bias of Bismarck's foreign policy. There were further arrangements, but all in all with the Romanian alliance the second and much more rigid phase of the system was completed.

The Achilles' heel of the system so far was the antagonism between Russia and Austria in the Balkans. When tension mounted again in 1886 it became impossible to keep both under the same roof. Another remodelling was imperative. So Bismarck

49

made new agreements, adding to or subtracting from the existing treaties exactly as he pleased.

With the beginning of 1887 the third phase began. At this time Bismarck was preoccupied with the possibility of a Franco-Russian alliance and he decided that the attempt to block Russia and isolate France should be continued by having others do the work. Bismarck himself could then reassure Russia, so that the temptation for Russia and France to ally would be minimized.

First of all, Rome took advantage of Austrian and German embarrassment to demand the activation of the triple alliance. Vienna was worried about Russian designs in the Balkans, and Berlin was uneasy about a flare-up of French chauvinism. Bismarck needed Italian co-operation, so he agreed to help, if Italy were militarily to resist a French advance into Libya. At the same time, Bismarck sought to lighten the new burden. He encouraged Britain and Italy to agree on the Mediterranean status quo. This they did and were joined by Austria and Spain. Thus, Bismarck had accepted greater responsibilities, but he had also succeeded in drawing Britain into the anti-French front – and into an anti-Russian front in the event of Russian aggression, since the entente on the Mediterranean referred to the Black Sea as well. Bismarck did not himself join these agreements so he was free to promise Russia help, knowing that she could attempt nothing. This is exactly what he did in the reinsurance treaty of 1887, which was designed to replace the Three Emperors' League after it had finally dissolved. In return, Russia promised neutrality in a Franco-German war so long as Germany was not the aggressor. This promise was less generous than the unqualified pledge of neutrality in force during the Three Emperors' League (1881–7), but it did prevent Russian support for French belligerence and that was the main aim.

This network of treaties and agreements is what most historians mean when they refer to the Bismarck system. Bismarck's disciples admire the complexity and effectiveness of the web; his critics argue that the various strands were a mere tangle and that in a crisis it would be useless. But they all point to the importance of the agreements constituting the system.

Perhaps the network was not the essence of his foreign policy, but merely one aspect. Bismarck's system-making appears out of character. If we look at the core and not the trappings, his policy before and after 1870–1 was not so very different. Indeed, the key to an understanding of his foreign policy after 1871 is his desire for balanced tension. He seemed to believe that German security and manoeuvrability would be most strongly guaranteed by creating and perpetuating tension between other powers. The alliance system was one means of attaining this end. The real Bismarck system – if such we may call it – was the creation or perpetuation of a fluid state of affairs in which tension was finely balanced and friends as well as opponents were immobilized.

Bismarck's approach was more dynamic and imaginative than is usually realized. He made use of formal agreements, but resorted to other strategies as well. There was first of all the occasional crude threat, direct or indirect, of force. When allies seemed to be growing too intimate he would stimulate suspicion amongst them. He was not beyond limited co-operation with his ostensible enemies in order to remind friends of the consequences should he become irrevocably estranged. \He could slander a lukewarm friend – the press or any other direct means was suitable for this. Now and then he could also apply direct pressure on an unco-operative government. In the 1860s he had made some use of overall economic policy in foreign affairs. In the 1870s and 1880s he was less inclined to do this, but he was quite prepared to use the small bore weapon of administrative regulations. If he thought his friends might fall out, he tried to avoid war, but in such a way as to prevent complete reconciliation. He acted sometimes as mediator, although he was temperamentally unsuited to play that role. There was also the apparently more affable side to his activity. Foreign diplomats could imbibe his wine and wisdom; his repeated hints to them about alliances were meant partly as a probe and partly as bait. They worked up to a point, but by raising expectations which had to be dashed, they achieved very little in the long run.

In all this sometimes hectic, and always wide-ranging, activity, the alliance net was but one element. If we focus on it, we miss the essence of Bismarckian diplomacy. Indeed the policy of balancing tension was in many respects the antithesis of a system.

If we look at Bismarck's policy after the Treaty of Frankfurt (1871) in this way, the strands of continuity with the earlier period emerge more clearly. And the apparently puzzling change from bellicosity to benevolence is explained. We see continuing ingenuity, restlessness, vigour and abrasiveness. As well as this we see the uncertainty as to goals and tactics, and the temptation of opportunism. But the function or purpose of this imaginative policy was different. In the 1860s Bismarck was more concerned with guiding and encouraging the forces of expansion and change; after 1871 he began to apply the brakes.

6 Bismarck, the Catholics and the Workers: the Limits of Power

The political groups which dominated the empire disappeared with it. Those parties then almost beyond the pale of civilization, the Catholics and socialists, dominate Germany today. If the measure of a man is his ability to pick the winners in tomorrow's race, Bismarck's score is low. Looked at from the Catholic and socialist point of view, the sore points of Bismarck's domestic policy are painfully apparent: he misunderstood and mishandled both groups. But if we assume a conservative, liberal or democratic stance the problems are much greater. In a sense, the constitution and the reform work of the 1870s amounted to an attempt to reconcile these groups with one another. And he was not altogether unsuccessful. Concessions to the Catholics and workers in the 1880s were sensible, even imaginative. But they did not work, not only because Bismarck had been more unkind to them than others who felt abused as well, but also because the pull of traditional Prussia or the new empire was too weak to allow them to forgive and forget.

The fairly common belief today that Bismarck's empire was a haven for aristocrats is quite untrue. In the early 1870s most of them surely looked on him as a Jacobin of sorts. Soon many felt that the new empire had its advantages, and they had the realism to see that more could be saved by co-operation than by opposition. Nevertheless, those of us who regard Bismarck as a junker, an outright representative of the gentry, will have to account for the disenchantment of these people with his reforms: the parliament with extensive powers, public debates and

53

universal manhood suffrage, the secret ballot for imperial elections, liberal economic and legal reforms, the secularization of the state, even the very existence of the empire. Its institutions looked very middle-class and so increasingly did the ethos of its people. Eley and Blackbourn have pointed to this. Indeed the spirit of the time in Germany was moving strongly away from aristocratic to middle-class society and values. The imperial Government was not responsible to parliament and the army reserve officer seemed to be omnipotent, yet Germany was surely changing rapidly, probably more rapidly than either France or Britain.

Although the ranks of the radicals and democrats in imperial Germany were thin, liberals of various hues were legion. They all wanted parliamentary instead of merely constitutional government. Most did not want reform to go further than this. And since they could all agree that the new empire was virtually a nation-state, and that therefore half their aspirations had been satisfied, the spirit of realism led them, as well as the conservatives to accept, willingly, the new arrangements.

On balance, the empire was an inspired compromise. It was conservative and federal enough to appease society's traditional leaders; it was sufficiently liberal and national to win over the middle-classes. The office of chancellor was also tailor-made for Bismarck, giving him power, responsibility and standing. In this way most of those who mattered were accommodated.

Two apparently less important social groups, the Catholics and the workers were overlooked, and therefore less thrilled by Bismarck's achievement. What was his approach to these two groups? We may discard at the outset the current popular notion that Bismarck sought to unite the rest of the country by persecuting German outsiders. This is in line with the view that nothing unites a country like a splendid and successful small-scale war – even if it is a civil war. Quite apart from the fact that if this was Bismarck's ploy, it did not work; he had other and more obvious things in mind.

During the 1870s the institutions of the empire were set up along liberal lines and middle-class values made rapid headway. The 1880s were, as they almost had to be, a period of retrenchment. It would be false to read too much into the conservative shift in Bismarck's politics at the end of the 1870s since during that decade he was no more liberal than he was conservative in the 1880s, but the two decades are indeed distinct.

In the 1870s the strengthening of imperial unity under his firm guidance was Bismarck's main goal. The liberals also wanted a compact empire and thought that by co-operating with the Government they could fashion it according to their own beliefs and then nudge Bismarck out: the progress of the liberal spirit would lead to parliamentary control over the Government. As we know this was not achieved until the empire was defeated in war in 1918. Treitschke was one of the few who foresaw this. He wrote in August 1866 that Caesarism would surely not yield soon to a parliamentary spirit. But toward the end of the 1870s, the liberals felt that the time for a trial of strength had come. Had the series of reforms continued, they were virtually certain to succeed. That is why Bismarck was determined to call a halt to them. His countrymen were fairly easily persuaded that this was the right course. After all, change had been rapid and, since the economy had been depressed since 1873, it looked as if liberalism had brought this about – or at any rate worsened matters – and that something else should be tried. The 1880s then, were conservative in spirit and there was a return to strong government and a movement away from *laissez-faire*. But there was in some ways a new departure also. Government intervention in the economy went further than before and looks in some ways very modern to us today. So too does the experiment in state socialism. Thus it could be argued that the conservative 1880s were in fact more modern than the previous liberal decade.

If we turn now to those two aspects of Bismarck's domestic policy which have been most heavily criticized we can see the extent and limitations of his achievement, the effect of his combative approach to politics. We shall look first at the *kulturkampf*, and then at the social quesion.

The kulturkampf

Since the early Middle Ages, relations between the Catholic

55

Church and the state had been at the centre of European history. There had been repeated struggles for ascendancy or influence. The growth of materialism in the nineteenth century forced a rapid adjustment in several countries, and none of these were painless. In Prussia the dispute bears the name of *kulturkampf*, a word coined by Rudolf Virchow (a talented physician, speaker and Liberal), meaning a struggle for civilization and humanity. It would have been unusual had there been no friction. What is interesting is the form it took.

It seems that the Church was trying desperately to defend its interests against the rising tide of materialism. We can see this in the Papal 'Syllabus of Errors' (1864), a wholesale damnation of Liberalism, and even more in the declaration of infallibility which coincided with the opening of hostilities between France and Germany in July 1870. The struggles for Catholic spiritual unity and German political unity began simultaneously. The conviction that the two battles were in some way intimately connected was widespread. Rightly or wrongly, the defeat of France was regarded as a defeat for Catholicism.

German – and indeed European – public opinion was incensed by what looked like a papal attempt at universal monarchy. Resistance to the pope as well as to the French emperor seemed like a national duty. Bismarck appeared less concerned at first, yet he soon led the ranks against the Church. The founding of the Catholic Centre Party in December 1870 was the crucial event. Its aim was to defend the Roman Church; and it sought to do this by favouring a policy of decentralization. It was not established as an opposition party, but it nevertheless quickly attracted many who were disenchanted with the empire which was founded the following month. In Bismarck's eyes the party was suspect from the start. What worried him also was the support it received from Prussia's Poles. He regarded Polish nationalism and Catholicism as a potentially explosive mixture and was very concerned about the support it was bound to receive from other Germans. He decided to act. Initially he wanted to disentangle the state from the Church – to separate Church from state. He hoped that this would push back Polish and clerical influence in the eastern provinces and so reduce the likelihood of interference in the

56

state's domain. He apparently believed that the Centre Party either could not or would not resist. But it did, and so Bismarck became determined not only to separate state from Church, but to gain the upper hand over the Church. Pope Pius IX was as much a fighter as Bismarck. And so the struggle became a trial of strength which was personal as much as political. In attacking the Catholic Church, Protestant institutions were also damaged: both churches were upset by the withdrawal of their powers to supervise local schools – the state also regulated the education of the clergy and disciplinary procedures. Conservative circles in Prussia were particularly disenchanted.

The Church of Rome yielded no ground and lost no supporters. German liberals backed the anti-clerical line, as did liberals elsewhere. For instance, in 1874 Gladstone expressed approval of Bismarck's approach: 'I cannot but say that the present doctrines of the Roman church destroy the title of her obedient members to the enjoyment of civil rights' (Knaplund, 1944, p. 127). But towards the end of the 1870s, Bismarck was turning away from the liberals. What was the point in continued struggle with the Church if he separated from his main ally and approached those with sincere religious convictions? Early in 1878 Pius IX died and was succeeded by Leo XIII who was firm, but not immovable. A bargain could be reached on the basis of mutual concessions. On the international plane the situation had also changed. At the onset of the *kulturkampf* fear of a Catholic coalition was probably a secondary consideration for Bismarck. Following the fall of Thiers, a man of peace, in 1873, the French regime seemed more susceptible to religious considerations, and Bismarck's concern grew. But after the beginning of an extraordinarily bitter French *kulturkampf*, and the conclusion in 1879 of an alliance with Austria – the most Catholic of European states – and the gradual extension of the alliance net, the fear of Catholic intervention dwindled. So during the 1880s the tension was slowly reduced. Peace with the Church was concluded in 1887, but it was a political compromise which satisfied no one. The state's reputation for religious toleration had taken a knock, but otherwise it had won quite a bit of ground from both the Protestant and Catholic churches. Nevertheless, members of the two denominations were convinced that the state was becoming overmighty; each was also troubled by the suspicion that the other had gained more than it had given. Relations between the denominations, always precarious, took a turn for the worse. The state had ridden roughshod over the constitutional rights of its people. Many, unfortunately, approved of this in the interest of the general welfare. Others – Protestants as well as Catholics – did not. Their position may have been morally admirable, but they seemed ineffectual and, worse, their loyalty seemed other than purely German and therefore suspect. A point frequently overlooked is that relations between Christians and Jews also deteriorated during the *kulturkampf* and partly because of it. Many of the leading liberals were of the Jewish faith, so the dislike of Christians was transferred to them. During the *kulturkampf*, anti-semitism grew amongst Protestants and Catholics. Not only were German Catholics, Protestants and Jews set against themselves; Protestant Prussians found increasingly determined opposition from Catholic Poles. The *kulturkampf* was, and could only be, socially divisive.

Socialism

We turn now to Bismarck's attitude towards the socialists, that is, those who were beginning to assume the leadership of the workers' movement. The appearance in the nineteenth century of a large urban working class necessitated a social adjustment on an unprecedented scale. The strains on German society in the last half of the century were particularly acute because of the very rapid rate of industrialization, as well as the necessity for political adjustment resulting from unification. It is not surprising that the aim of integrating the workers into national life was not entirely successful. However, it was not a complete failure. Compared with workers in other countries the Germans were economically fairly well-off by 1914, and their relative position had improved over the previous decades. Their performance in the trenches bears comparison with men from other countries. We should be careful not to read too much into these facts, but what remains is that they obviously did not feel like complete social or national rejects. If Bismarck deserves much of the credit for the partially successful integration of the new working class, he also deserves much of the blame for what went wrong. How did he approach the question?

Industrialization came late to Germany, accelerated rapidly during the 1850s and 1860s and peaked from 1871 to 1873. Then the crash came. A twenty-three year period of relative depression followed. During the 1860s the working class had expanded; not only was it distinctly visible, but it also made up the greater part of the new industrial cities. The workers remained without political power, but they had enjoyed some of the benefits of the expanding economy. After the crash they felt that they suffered the full force of the ensuing depression. In fact those who remained in work did rather well; it was because their expectations had grown so unjustifiably high that the shock seemed so rude.

Parallel with this, the German labour movement began to develop. Rapid industrialization in the third quarter of the nineteenth century had created not only an industrial proletariat, but also a moderately wealthy middle-class convinced of the virtues of economic liberalism. When the depression came they sought relief through further liberal reforms and indeed the trade tariff was steadily reduced. The workers' leaders felt that a new departure was needed. Before the depression they had already formed two moderate workers' parties which united in 1875 to form the Social Democratic Party, a slightly more radical organization with an element of Marxism. Clearly, the political head of the workers' movement was becoming more radical. The liberals in parliament were prepared to do nothing either for or against them. Bismarck, more combative by nature, was sensitive to the experience of ancient Greece and Rome and the very much more recent experiences of France. During the commune rising in early 1871 he had been worried about the excesses of the masses and tried to organize a common conservative front against them. He probably felt this would isolate France even further, protect society against a real danger and also, somewhat conveniently, help him to shake off his own reputation as a trouble maker. His deep fear of revolution sprang also from a concern that his own German revolution could get out of control. These considerations applied at home in Germany during, and then after, the war with France. He was determined to strike out against the radical agitation of the proletariat or its leaders but was willing to give the workers some material assistance – he regarded them as urbanized, well-meaning and conservative former serfs in need of a helping hand from above. They could and should be saved from irresponsible leaders.

Bismarck's approach to what was quickly to become the most pressing social problem can be explained at the outset by reference to his own psychological make-up, his paternalistic background and a cluster of political fears and calculations. Despite what was probably a sincere wish to help, he did nothing of the kind during the 1870s. But he did take a fairly tough line with the socialist leaders and pressed parliament to be even harder. It could be argued that the liberals kept him from helping the poor. But why did they not, in keeping with their *laissez-faire* attitudes, prevent him from dealing firmly with the workers' prospective leaders? The obvious answer is probably correct: the liberals' fear of unrest was stronger than their own principles, and much the same could be said of Bismarck.

In 1878 there were two attempts on the emperor's life. At this time the socialists were visibly gaining in popularity, which was worrying. Still worse, the liberals were becoming more demanding. Bismarck saw the opportunity to kill two birds with one stone. The socialists were blamed for the attempted assassinations and a law against their activities was thrust through parliament. The law remained on the books until 1890, and while it did not ban the party as such, it did suppress its agitation. Most liberals were willing to keep the socialists in check using moderate measures. But the party split when it came to outright persecution. Bismarck succeeded in getting both the socialists and liberals where he wanted them. Having deprived the workers of their leaders and the liberals of their unity, he could make sure that his work could not be undone by proceeding then to an epoch-making new departure: the attempt to solve the social question through a state insurance scheme. We may wonder why he chose insurance rather than the more obvious methods of factory legislation or education.

In fact, the extraordinarily ambitious idea of comprehensive insurance met several needs. The workers would benefit considerably from the security offered by the state, and would therefore be profoundly grateful. They already out-numbered the middle-classes and, properly reassured, could also restrain them. The influence of the state and the chancellor would be enhanced and there would be possibilities for further influence. The determined resistance of the liberals to these proposals would increase their isolation. The *rapprochement* between Bismarck and Christian elements would be facilitated. This looks fairly clear with hindsight, but we must not forget that, judged by the conventional wisdom of the day, Bismarck's insurance idea was hare-brained and unworkable.

Bismarck was not sure whether his leap in the dark would be successful. The workers seemed surprisingly ungrateful so that his zest for further social reform flagged. Factory legislation would have involved interference in the relations between employer and employee to an extent which insurance did not and it looked as if he would reap only a harvest of recrimination. Bismarck was notoriously uninterested in education inasmuch as it went beyond practical instruction. Moreover, German workers were already much better educated than their contemporaries elsewhere. Improvements in primary education were therefore minor. However, major improvements were made in the practical aspects of secondary and tertiary education, although the workers did not benefit from them. If humanitarian concerns had been more than incidental with Bismarck, perhaps he would have pressed on with further reforms, but he was basically unconcerned about the lot of his blue-collared subjects in the factories or about their social mobility.

It might not be unfair to say that Bismarck himself had little understanding for what may well have been his most distinguished achievement. In the long run he did in fact come very close to reaching his initial goal: that of creating a pliable and contented workforce. But this was to come after the collapse of the empire, his apparently more grand but in fact more fragile accomplishment.

In assessing Bismarck's approach to the Catholics and the

socialists, we should, above all, be aware of the problems that he faced. In the late nineteenth century, conflict between the state and the church, and between the state and socialism was unavoidable. Given this fact, it is perhaps not surprising that he won over neither workers nor Catholics. Nevertheless, his policies towards both groups were to have important and far-reaching consequences.

7   The Social and Economic Interpretation of German History

As we have seen, Bismarck's political stance in the 1870s appears partly liberal and partly aggressive. During the 1880s his approach is both conservative and post-liberal, or ultra-modern. If we turn to his economic policy we see a similar pattern. The change from *laissez-faire* economics to protectionism, and then to imperialism, has been much discussed since the appearance of Böhme's book in 1966 and Wehler's in 1969. Since both authors deal with wider issues than their ostensible subjects, this may be the place to examine them even though we shall have to glance back to the 1850s and 1860s.

At the end of the 1870s Bismarck had a series of disputes with the liberals. The chancellor's pressure for a protective tariff occupied the centre of the stage and may well have been the key issue, contributing as it did to a split in the liberal ranks and precipitating an overall change in economic policy at home and abroad. It also fits neatly into an emerging pattern which can be interpreted in one way or another.

After 1873 the depressed economy had several deleterious effects. Not only were the new and over-expanded industries in difficulties but the imperial Government had trouble raising money to meet its obligations. A fiscal reform was mandatory. For Bismarck, the advantages of a tariff were obvious: it would produce revenue, help industry and, since wild annual fluctuation was undesirable, it would not easily be controlled by parliament. The other reason for a tariff, a general tariff – and this was dear to Bismarck – was that German agriculture had been under strain

63

for more than a generation. Fecklessness, poor harvests, increasing debts, smaller farms, and, since the late 1860s, competition from America and Russia, all took their toll. Previously Germany had exported grain – much of it to England. Agricultural machinery and other goods as well came by sea on the return journey. Landowners had been 'free traders', but the locomotive and steamer brought grain into Germany in the 1870s.

Bismarck was himself a landowner, and the advantage of an agricultural tariff did not escape him. So he wanted a tariff, (a) for fiscal and economic reasons: the Government would get revenues and industry as well as agriculture would be protected, (b) for political reasons: it would check and perhaps split the liberals; (c) for personal reasons: his own pocketbook would benefit, and his power vis-à-vis parliament would be strengthened. In Bismarck's eyes, therefore, the concept of a general tariff was of course not a panacea, but it was not much less either. Most historians would agree with what has been said, with differences of emphasis obviously. Böhme, however, has put forward views which are sufficiently different and interesting to warrant examination.

Böhme argues that the purpose of the tariff was to create a conservative welfare state by tying the large landowners and big business to the state in order to preserve the social status quo. This interpretation has the advantage of simplicity and appears convincing, but it attributes too much ideological consistency to Bismarck and overlooks the influence of tactical considerations and personal idiosyncrasies. Böhme believes that upper-class solidarity created by the tariff and the socialist law, precarious though it might have been, nevertheless established a front against the working classes which was maintained till 1918 (and it was in fact this senseless confrontation which doomed Germany). Bismarck's foreign policy can also be explained by the need to maintain this conservative welfare state. Böhme sees 1879 as a pivotal point in German history. On 18 January 1871 the political framework of the empire was built. In 1879 the social structure and political hierarchy were solidified, and this was vastly more important. Böhme believes in the prime importance of economic issues even before 1879; afterwards economic considerations dictated the course of German history. This seems something of a misreading of events and does not tally with the effect of other aspects of Bismarck's foreign and domestic policy. For instance, in the 1880s Bismarck ended the *kulturkampf* and backed the seminal social insurance scheme. Böhme also minimizes to an intolerable degree the meaning for contemporaries of the ceremony in the Hall of Mirrors: for them the ceremony was an act of almost religious significance. Taking a more limited assessment of Bismarck's motives, we can say that in the short term he achieved most of what he wanted. The imperial finances were put on a sound footing; industry and agriculture received some support. The liberal party was torn apart and its dominance ended for good. Bismarck's own position and that of the state were enhanced.

Since the German general tariff was an abrupt reversal of previous policy and gave a good deal of impetus to the protectionist movement everywhere, perhaps we ought to ask what its tangible results were. The short answer is that we do not know. Protectionists argue that it was in line with the trend of the day, and point to the unmistakable turn for the better afterwards. They claim that as the tariff wall mounted, so too did prosperity. Free traders, however, underline the very slow recovery, and lament the almost universal race for tariff protection. Regrettable as the turn to protection may have been for liberals, one must not dramatize its ill-effects. Rosenberg's view that it discouraged agricultural modernization by aiding carefree landowners is correct, up to a point. But on the other hand, a failure to protect agriculture would have led to worse conditions for many in the countryside and encouraged even more emigration to the cities where conditions were also difficult. The tariff therefore should not be regarded as an attempt to unite the establishment (some of whom were free traders) against the workers (many of whom benefited from it).

Not only have Böhme's views on the significance of the tariff been widely discussed recently, so too have other aspects of his interpretation of German history. He is a pupil of Fritz Fischer, and one of Fischer's major contributions to the study of this period is the notion that events at home were very important for the formation of foreign policy. This may not sound very new, but German historians since Ranke have insisted that in their country, foreign policy took precedence over affairs at home. This is the doctrine of the 'primacy of foreign policy'. Taking his cue from Fischer, Böhme argues for the 'primacy of domestic policy'.

Böhme would disagree with the slant of this study, holding that we must not see the history of the foundation of the German empire and its first two decades as part of Bismarck's biography, but just the reverse. Bismarck did not make Germany; Germany made Bismarck. This is a point well worth considering as is his belief that we ought carefully to examine the economic and social factors because they were of major importance. He argues forcefully that German unity emerged from Prussia's counter measures against Austria's political and economic policy on Central Europe after 1848. Both countries tried to guide the national movement for selfish purposes. The point is that the truly creative work was done well before 1862 and not afterwards. The crucial period was between 1849 and 1864, during which time Prussia manoeuvred Austria out of the German economy. So the dates of Bismarck's three wars: 1864, 1866, 1870, and the deeds of his generals, do not really matter so much. After about 1865 German unity was more or less inevitable, but not because Bismarck cut short his vacation in September 1862.

Since neither economic nor political issues decide themselves, and Böhme does not believe in heroes, he points to the work of an anti-hero, Rudolf von Delbrück, who in a way personifies all that was best in the Prussian administration. He, representing the bureaucracy, a mere privy counsellor in the ministry of trade, successfully met the Austrian challenge in the 1850s. Later (in 1867) Delbrück became head of the federal and later imperial chancellery and remained there for nine years. He was then the vice chancellor, in fact if not in name, and as such he established the imperial institutions on a solid and reasonably liberal footing. Inasmuch as imperial Germany was in tune with the times, this was Delbrück's accomplishment. Even for these enormous services Delbrück has not received his due. We must thank Böhme for reminding us that Bismarck did not stand alone. The trouble is that Delbrück's role in the 1850s and early 1860s looks much less important than it was to be later on, and it might be best not to elevate him too much. Delbrück's idea was simple: after surviving the trauma of 1848 the Austrians sought to strengthen their state by working for a central European customs union which they could dominate. High tariffs were needed so that Austria could prosper. Prussia and the rest of the customs union did not need or want high duties. So Delbrück, who was a free trader, unswervingly opposed them. Prussia's liberal trade policy and her downward spiralling tariffs were followed willy-nilly by the other German states. South Germans preferred Vienna to Berlin, but they knew which side their bread was buttered.

In economic matters, Prussia was consistently liberal through-out the 1850s. The rest of her domestic policy was entirely reactionary. In foreign affairs she lacked direction. Only in her economic policy, master-minded by Delbrück, were there signs of intelligence and vigour. The Prussian economy prospered; the Austrian economy also expanded, but fell behind in relative terms. By the end of the 1850s, Prussia seemed more qualified for leadership than Austria which had lost a war, was losing itself in constitutional experiments, and seemed set to lose the economic race.

Böhme believes that the crucial change in Prussia's indecisive foreign policy came with the appointment of Count Bernstorff as foreign minister in 1861, because he and not his successor, Bismarck, introduced a tough approach based on a realistic appraisal of true Prussian interests, *realpolitik*. Delbrück brought the great change in economic affairs; Bernstorff did the same in foreign policy. Bismarck's line was more that of an epigone rather than an innnovator. Bernstorff's approach emerged out of Prussia's experience in 1859. During the war of that year, Austrian weakness and isolation were painfully clear, and Prussia had the opportunity to forge ahead. One of his accomplishments was the preparation of a liberal trade agreement with France which protectionist Austria could not join but the rest of Germany could. This agreement was finalized just before Bismarck took office.

Another important project, begun before Bismarck became

prime minister, was the reform of the army. Mobilization in 1859 had uncovered serious failings which the new measures sought to remedy. The iron chancellor therefore inherited much from his predecessors. He appeared at the critical moment and fought the battle to a successful conclusion. If we accept this reading of events, 1859 and 1861 were perhaps more fateful years than 1864, 1866 or 1870. This is surely worth pondering and helps us to put Bismarck's achievement in perspective. But one has the feeling that Delbrück is slightly more convincing as an unsung or anti-hero than Bernstorff who was little more than a well-schooled traditional diplomat. The ruthless energy of Bismarck was profoundly different.

Böhme writes that when Bismarck moved into the government offices in Wilhelmstrasse\he tried to rule with 'iron and blood'; but it was even more important to base his policy on iron and coal. He sought political ascendancy by obtaining and using Prussia's economic ascendancy. This, the secret to his success, he had discovered from his predecessors. But, sadly, most of the *zollverein* was on the Austrian side in 1866.

Having emphasized that Bismarck's wars and his diplomacy are less significant than is often argued, Böhme contends, finally, that the political foundation of the empire was also not the milestone in European history that it is supposed to be. It was a by-product of economic policy which itself led to the real social and economic founding of the empire in 1878–9 with the adoption of a tariff uniting the wealthy in town and country in defence of the political and social status quo.

Here we have an alternative to the standard political interpretations of German history which carefully focus on Bismarck. We can, if we like, adopt much of what Böhme suggests for he has added new dimensions to our understanding of this period. Yet the impression left by his book is that this approach is as lopsided as the purely biographical explanation of German unification: if men are not entirely free agents, it is also true to say that they do not live by bread alone, and history is not a derivative of economics.

That Germany should have been caught up in the surge of imperialism during the 1880s is not surprising, especially since the country had abandoned her free trade policy after the introduction of the tariff. But Bismarck's motives are not quite so clear as the casual observer might think. More than anything his abrupt departure into imperialism startled contemporaries and puzzled historians.

At the beginning of the 1870s, Bismarck had likened German colonies to the silky fur coats of Polish noblemen who possessed no shirts (*G.W.*, vii, no. 388). On many occasions he discouraged colonists from expecting government support; and at the end of the 1880s he insisted that he had never been keen to follow imperialist policies. Was all this mere diversion or hypocrisy? It seems safe to say that Bismarck was never really a colonial enthusiast. In the late 1870s he firmly believed that colonial ties drained national power; he was therefore glad to see the French show an interest in imperialist expansion which he thought would weaken them. At the same time, however, German commercial activity was expanding and Bismarck was willing to grant legal and consular protection. As early as 1874 there was a squabble with Britain over Fiji. This small incident showed that if German commerce was to develop further more protection would be needed. The German merchants had had a thriving business in Fiji and they felt that by annexing the islands, the British had trampled on their interests. Towards the end of the 1870s Bismarck began to stand up more for the rights of German merchants abroad. It would have been surprising had he not done this. The enactment of the tariff offering protection at home suggested protection abroad as well. But this was not enough to convince him that Germany needed colonies.

Fifty years ago Townsend surveyed German colonial policy. She believed then, and others since have thought along similar lines, that Bismarck was converted to imperialism at an early stage and carefully worked towards the establishment of a colonial empire. There are indeed some scraps of evidence to substantiate this view, but little more than that. It seems wiser to seek explanations for a change in Bismarck's attitude in the early 1880s.

The significance of the tariff and the legacy of minor colonial disputes in the 1870s have already been mentioned. Two other factors influenced Bismarck when he finally strove to establish a colonial empire in 1883–5. First of all the international situation was favourable. Germany was protected by the triple alliance and the Three Emperors' League. Relations with Turkey and Spain were also good. And, of greater importance yet, France and Britain, the two leading colonial powers, were quarrelling over Egypt which Britain had just occupied. The French, surprisingly, looked to Germany for support. Resistance to German colonial expansion could only come from an isolated Britain. Gladstone, the prime minister, was not necessarily opposed to the Germans acquiring colonies although unfortunately this message did not get through to Berlin. The opportunity as a whole looked good. This was an important consideration for anyone like Bismarck who had a short-term view of diplomacy and a sharp eye for any new opening.

Not only were the circumstances auspicious; the colonial movement had begun to make rapid headway. The desire for colonies was growing all over Europe, including Germany. When Bismarck made the first moves towards creating Germany's empire parliament and public opinion still opposed expansion. The trend in Germany as elsewhere, however, was strongly towards imperialism. The arguments of the German colonial movement were essentially the same as in other countries. Economic considerations occupied the foreground of the public discussion. There were, however, numerous other concerns, ranging from those based on the widespread opinion that Germany suffered from excess population, to considerations of national prestige and humanitarian and religious beliefs. The sincerity of the colonial enthusiasts cannot be questioned, but in addition to those with elevated motives there were also rogues and others who were simply looking for adventure.

Ever since the Congress of Berlin in 1878 the rivalry for colonies had been intensifying. The energies of the major European peoples began to sail forth from the haven of their own states and out into a larger sea where there was increasingly fierce competition for prestige and power. The scramble for colonies was well underway when Bismarck's ships came over the horizon. Robinson and Gallagher, however, attribute it to German intervention; this is clearly a misjudgement, but it is the case that the scramble became more hectic with the appearance of a new competitor.

Bismarck would not have sought to acquire colonies had he thought this move would have been unpopular at home. But the energetic action of several Bremen and Hamburg merchants was more important because it forced him to take a stand.

This explanation of the change in Bismarck's attitude towards colonial expansion is fairly unobjectionable as far as it goes, but some have not been satisfied with references to the colonial movement (at home and abroad) and the auspicious international situation. From this point of view, Bismarck looks like an outright opportunist without goals of his own. Indeed, Taylor's account runs along these lines. He adds that Bismarck wanted to pick a fight with Britain in order to form an entente with France (1938). We know that relations with France did improve briefly at this time, while relations with Britain deteriorated. But this was surely the price Bismarck had to pay for success abroad and it probably did not occur to him that the residual irritation in the Foreign Office would outlast what could only be a temporary improvement in relations with France. Had the thought crossed his mind, it might not have caused him much anxiety for the following reason. William I, the emperor, was very old and the heir apparent was pro-English. Should relations with Britain worsen, the successor to the throne would be compelled to follow a more pro-Russian line. This would be ideal because William I was too pro-Russian for Bismarck; his successor, Frederick III, was too pro-English – a compromise would be just right. This is the view advanced by Eyck in his monumental biography. The chancellor must have thought of it, but it scarcely looks like a convincing major reason for the departure into colonial policy.

Since the publication of his book in 1969, Wehler has dominated the discussion on imperialism, and is in some respects

71

closer to the truth than his predecessors; even where he is not his views have been so influential that they warrant attention. Wehler, a Marxist of sorts, sees two roots to Bismarck's imperialism: (a) the Great Depression and Bismarck's rather pragmatic attempts to overcome it (the economic root); and (b) social imperialism. For Wehler this is the attempt to preserve the old social structure of Germany by creating an attractive but irrelevant distraction. Wehler carefully elaborates both these arguments, but the concept of social imperialism is closest to his heart.

He believes that German imperialism grew on German soil. The favourable international scene merely occasioned the found-ation of a formal empire. The theories about imperialism resulting from international rivalry or the collapse of African regimes mean little to him. Turning first to the economic source of German imperialism, Wehler argues that it was a response to the depression which stretched from 1873 to 1896. Like other statesmen, Bismarck attempted to combat the recession by a series of *ad hoc* measures to stimulate the economy: he extended consular protection, and subsidized shipping in order to facilitate exports. Wehler argues that Bismarck consistently backed Prussian and German trade from 1862 onwards, that he believed in an informal colonial empire throughout, and that the establishment of a formal empire in the 1880s represented only a small change. Seeing the origin of German colonialism as part of the attempt to break out of a stubborn depression makes sense and fits into a pattern of reactions throughout society – the move towards concentration and co-operation amongst similar groups against outsiders. This was accompanied by an analogous psychological reaction – the dislike of social outsiders such as Jews was greatly increased. Wehler's attempt to show continuity in Bismarck's colonial aspirations is less successful. The backing for foreign trade until the 1880s was sporadic. In addition, the change-over from informal methods of domination to a formal empire does not in fact seem to be a difference in gradation but rather of kind.

The most original and contentious aspect of Wehler's work is his theory of social imperialism. Like Napoleon, Bismarck is

72

supposed to have sought victory abroad to solve trouble at home. That is, in order to preserve the stratified German social and political structure, he embarked upon foreign adventure which, he also hoped, would give the home economy a boost – the old formula of food and fun for the masses. For Wehler this attitude was not only behind Bismarck's colonial policy but the new imperialism generally, and certainly behind German foreign policy from Bismarck to Hitler. Wehler has no trouble illustrating his dubious view with various statements by a range of statesmen and it certainly has the virtue of clarity. Unfortunately it does not bear close scrutiny. There were, for instance, those who sought social change through imperial expansion and this was logically a more promising line to follow. But there were, and are, more tangible and obvious reasons for expansion. And Bismarck, who had a reputation for frankness, never said that he wanted colonies to keep the workers quiet. Why not? The answer is simply that imperialism was not a sensible means of achieving this goal. It could and did undermine the social structure. It was advocated by and benefited the urban middle-classes; the workers dependent on them were also beneficiaries. However, the interests and values of the landed aristocracy suffered. But this state of affairs was not Bismarck's primary goal either. Neither he nor any of the other leading statesmen of his day would have looked for colonies had they firmly believed that by so doing they would weaken the social and political status quo. Bismarck surely realized that this was a danger, but believed he could cope with it.

It is often said that Bismarck's colonial policy was a function of his European policy. In other words, his colonial policy had a low priority. This is probably true. However, the colonial expansion caused trouble with Britain and compromised his position in Europe. It reawakened suspicions of him. He knew how vulnerable colonies would be in war and certainly regarded them as pawns. He probably did not realize that his countrymen would in time find it difficult to regard the colonies and colonial policy dispassionately. Bismarck was uninterested in a fleet, but was it not likely that his successors would want a larger fleet to protect the colonies and trade in general? Wehler is wrong in postulating a consensus in Germany in favour of imperialist expansion during

73

Bismarck's term of office. But the colonial movement continued to grow and sacrifice became hard.

Given the growing attachment to the colonial empire, in the long run imperialism made Germany more vulnerable. Previously there was little reason for trouble with Britain. With colonies there would be a greater likelihood of conflict. The Germans saw once again the advantages which could accrue from an energetic policy. But others, the English, for instance, began to believe that Germany was too willing to use force and blackmail in foreign policy. The famous memorandum written a generation later in January 1907 by Eyre Crowe, an influential foreign office official, shows that this was no passing pique. Of course, if we look at it from a German angle, the British attitude was not above reproach. It seemed to be both imperious and ineffective – a bad combination. The memory of the years 1884–5, when virtually the whole of the German colonial empire was acquired, lingered on in the foreign offices of London and Berlin with unfortunate results for both countries.

Towards the end of the last century many people thought that the expansion of colonial empires and the rivalries between them were to be the challenge and opportunity of the twentieth century. It is no wonder that a growing and powerful people should want to compete. It would have been difficult, but not impossible, to opt out and at the same time avoid the complacent attitudes leading to decline. Indeed, an ostensibly less ambitious policy might well have brought greater rewards at lower cost, but for this line statesmanship was required.

8 Assessment

On Bismarck's retirement from office in March 1890, a cartoon in the humorous English journal, *Punch*, depicted the 'dropping of the pilot'. The European chancelleries did not celebrate his departure. He was unloved, it is true, but his astuteness and realism were universally appreciated, and there was widespread unease in Europe as to the future course of German foreign policy. And this unease was justified because not only was the pilot changed; so too was the vessel. Out went sail; in came steam. The new ship of state was impressive, but as we know, seamanship was wanting. If other countries were uneasy about Bismarck's resignation, the Germans were not. The pugnacious old man was becoming increasingly unpopular and most of his countrymen welcomed his departure.

William I and his successor Frederick III had both died in 1888. William II, the new emperor, was young and headstrong. Early in 1890 he and Bismarck had a series of clashes on a range of subjects. Behind them was a trial of wills which William won. Exactly what was at stake no one outside the government knew, but with the resignation of Bismarck people felt the promise of better and easier times. One of Bismarck's rivals, Ludwig Bamberger, put it this way: 'it is misfortunate that his departure is fortunate' (Feder, p. 66). Hopes were soon to be disappointed, however. When the meandering brashness of the new regime became apparent, the Bismarck cult mushroomed. Before his death in 1898 he was probably at the peak of his popularity. The reverence for the man was partly personal homage; it was also an expression of nostalgia.

Bismarck, whose achievements were so impressive and who

dominated politics for nearly thirty years, left a void on his departure. The new leaders had been kept firmly in their place and had little standing amongst their countrymen. They had to prove their ability and wisdom. They did not succeed in this, and although the chancellor has been criticized for failing to train his successors, it was their fault not his. In the rough and tumble of politics it is for every man to teach himself. No system of government has succeeded in assuring an unbroken succession of talent at the top. If we want to assess the impact of the man on his country, we must look deeper.

Bismarck taught Germans to see things coolly without paying much attention to morality. He showed them how to forget idealism and to regard idealists as hypocrits or rascals. He saw politics as a struggle for power and he taught men how to succeed without being consistent. His methods and goals were a demonic mixture of good and evil – a temptation and warning to both successors and the public alike. Herein lies the personal legacy of the shrewd and irascible genius. It was the gift of Prometheus.

Bismarck's frequent appearance in uniform was a pose. He gained respect through association with the victorious army, and the soldiers too won distinction from him. The military posturing also underlined the more belligerent aspects of his action. The man of 'blood and iron' was prominent; the diplomat was not. The reputation that this encouraged was an asset since few dared to oppose him and he could indulge in highly personalized feuds with those who tried to stand up to him. He made opposition look like treason. The lesson conveyed was that firmness of purpose and toughness in action succeed. But that these things were, and should be, controlled by a sense of realism was not so apparent and was less appreciated. Bismarckians like Treitschke understood the more popular and conspicuous aspects of their hero: they could see the man on horseback, but not the diplomat in evening dress.

Bismarck must be given credit for the unification of Germany. An empire of similar size and shape may well have emerged sooner or later, but the constitutional design was his. The delicate balance between centralism and federalism, between the forces of

recurring misgivings – they were convinced that Germans could do whatever they set their minds to do.

Pessimism ran straight through the main aspects of Bismarck's foreign as well as domestic policy, and helped him to a realistic appraisal of political life. He understood men's baser motives and could react accordingly. This was clearly an asset in diplomacy. However, since he sold idealism at a discount, he weakened the 'vital centre' of his own policy: he could not appreciate that the idealism of others was sometimes genuine. Bismarck's almost undiluted pessimism grated on the nerves of his associates and countrymen, but they nevertheless grew accustomed to it and in time became virtual converts. They were never quite as pessimistic or cynical as Bismarck, but they lacked his good sense and appreciation for the true interests of Germany and of others, and their foreign policy after his departure was abrasive and unsound.

Bismarck's attention to tactics was due in part to his pessimistic cast of mind. He had little hope for the future and firmly believed that the problem just ahead should have priority over that which lay on the horizon. He was, of course, a skilled tactician, but as I have tried to show in my study *Bismarck at the Crossroads* (1974), the real Bismarck was a great deal more fallible than legend has it. Bismarck's successors also paid great attention to tactics and were firmly convinced that somehow they would wriggle through as Bismarck had. They overlooked the fact that Bismarck frequently got himself into unnecessary trouble through pointless manoeuvrings, and that long-lasting antipathy would be engendered by tactical twists and turns.

Bismarck's policy of balanced tensions was never understood and was the first part of his approach to be thrown overboard. When he left office, the Russians wanted the renewal of the reinsurance treaty which had been concluded for three years in 1887. Such a treaty was not easily reconcilable with Germany's commitment to Austria and appeared to clash with that to Romania, so that in the interest of clarity and honesty and because of the general suspicion of the Russians it was dropped. Though the Russians were still willing to accept a less impressive agreement, this was also refused. Relations with the tsar had been deteriorating throughout the 1880s, but it was foolish in the extreme to alienate him, thus encouraging Russia to develop ties with France. Bismarck's 'system' of balanced tensions, with Berlin as the magnetic centre, was almost immediately replaced by two opposing blocs. In such a situation, an imperfect imitation of 'Bismarckian' politics (which was designed to operate in a very tense but freer atmosphere) was bound to fail – and it did.

Bismarck's Europe-oriented policy would have been doomed by 1900, even if its architect had remained healthy and in office until then. Berlin would have declined as the centre of European tensions, whether or not Germany wanted to become a world power; other states had either a stronger home base or a more extensive empire. After the departure of Bismarck, however, it was likely that Germany would strive to become such a power. There were many who felt that they understood the essence of his politics although they did not. They had none of Bismarck's gnawing doubts about German strength. They felt that the great chancellor had only done half the task. It was for them to do the rest; it would be a betrayal of their inheritance if they did not try to extend German power further – in proportion to Bismarck's own extension of Prussian power. In 1895 Max Weber argued that German unification was to be seen as an expensive childish escapade of an ageing nation which should have been avoided if it was intended as the termination and not the beginning of German world politics. It was not the dream of a power fanatic, but a sincere conviction shared by many and comprehensible to all.

If we look for strands of continuity from Bismarck to the Wilhelmine period and beyond, we can find them in many spheres. Some of these have already been pointed out. There were, however, vast differences. Wilhelmine Germany was energetic and prosperous – the economy was sluggish during Bismarck's last sixteen years in office. As early as 1872, he had said: 'I recently imagined the map of Germany: on it one rotting speck after another appeared and dropped off' (*G.W.*, viii, no. 33). His successors were less fearful. They were more self-confident and brash. Technology was vastly improved. But Germany was led by men who tried to emulate a Bismarck they did not understand, and who tried to apply imperfectly learned lessons in a situation totally different from that in which Bismarck had worked. The warnings of those who expressed fear that all was not well went unheeded. Bismarck's legacy was complex, and in 1890 or 1898 no one could say which aspects would be the most relevant either in 1914 or 1933.

References and Further Reading

The asterisk denotes books particularly useful for students.

Anderson, E. N. 1954: *The Social and Political Conflict in Prussia, 1858–1864*. Lincoln, Nebraska.

Bismarck, O. 1901: *Gedanken und Erinnerungen, Anhang*, 2 vols. Stuttgart.

Bismarck, O. 1924–35: *Die Gesammelten Werke*, 15 vols. Berlin. An indispensable collection of political writings, letters, speeches, table talk and memoirs.

Blackbourn, D. & Eley, G. 1984: *The Peculiarities of German History. Bourgeois Society and Politics in Nineteenth Century Germany*. Oxford.

Blanke, R. 1981: *Prussian Poland in the German Empire*. New York.

Böhme, H. 1966: *Deutschlands Weg zur Grossmacht*. Cologne. An important, debatable new view, confusingly presented.

*Böhme, H. 1967: Big business pressure groups and Bismarck's turn to protectionism. *Historical Journal*, 10. A summary of his long German book.

*Böhme, H. (ed.) 1971: *The Foundation of the German Empire: Select Documents*. Oxford. Contains important commentaries.

Bonnin, G. (ed.) 1957: *Bismarck and the Hohenzollern Candidature for the Spanish Throne: The Documents in the German Diplomatic Archives*. London. A vital collection with a revealing introduction concerning the history of the documents.

Busch, M. 1898: *Bismarck: Some Secret Pages of his History*, 3 vols. London. An accurate record of conversations with Bismarck which for years was regarded with suspicion.

*Carr, W. 1969: *A History of Germany, 1815–1945*. London. The best brief survey.

*Chamberlain, M. E. 1974: *The Scramble for Africa*. London. An excellent introduction.

Craig, G. 1955: *The Politics of the Prussian Army, 1640–1945*. Oxford.

*Craig, G. 1978: *Germany, 1866–1945*. Oxford. A full and balanced survey, superbly written.

Documents Diplomatiques Français. 1929 ff: (ed.) Ministère des Affaires Étrangères. Paris. Excellent French collection.

Eyck, E. 1941–4: *Bismarck: Leben und Werk*, 3 vols. Zurich. A brilliant liberal interpretation. Still the best thorough narrative.

*Eyck, E. 1948: *Bismarck after Fifty Years*. London. A distillation of the 3 vol. work.

Feder, E. (ed.) 1932: *Bismarcks grosses Spiel. Die geheimen Tagebücher Ludwig Bambergers*. Frankfurt.

Gall, L. 1980: *Bismarck. Der Weisse Revolutionär*. Frankfurt. By far the best full biography. More discussion than narrative.

Gifford, P. and Louis, W. R. (eds) 1967: *Britain and Germany in Africa*. New Haven, Connecticut.

Die Grosse Politik der Europäischen Kabinette. 1922–27: Lepsius, J. *et al.* (eds) The standard selection of official papers. The first six volumes cover the period till Bismarck's retirement.

Hamerow, T. S. 1969–72: *The Social Foundations of German Unification*, 2 vols. Princeton. A comprehensive and reliable account.

Henderson, W. O. 1939: *The Zollverein*. Cambridge.

Hillgruber, A. 1972: *Bismarcks Aussenpolitik*. Freiburg. An indispensable and concise discussion.

*Holborn, H. 1969: *A History of Modern Germany, 1840–1945*. New York. The best detailed survey but without references.

Kennedy, P. M. 1980: *The Rise of the Anglo-German Antagonism, 1860–1914*. London. Excellent.

*Kent, G. O. 1978: *Bismarck and his Times*. Carbondale, Illinois. A brief factual introduction with a concise discussion of the historical debate.

Kissinger, H. A. 1968: The white revolutionary: reflections on Bismarck. *Daedalus*, 97.

Knaplund, P. (ed.) 1944: *Letters from the Berlin Embassy*. Washington.

Lambi, I. N. 1963: *Free Trade and Protection in Germany, 1868–1879*. Wiesbaden. Deals with the background of the German general tariff.

*Langer, W. L. 1931: *European Alliances and Alignments*, New York. Still the best survey of international relations, but uncritical of Bismarck.

*Lidtke, V. 1966: *The Outlawed Party. Social Democracy in Germany, 1878–1890*. Princeton. The best study on the subject.

Marcks, E. 1915: *Bismarcks Jugend 1815–1848*. Stuttgart. Excellent.

Medlicott, W. N. 1938: *The Congress of Berlin and After*. London. Definitive on the Congress.

Medlicott, W. N. 1956: *Bismarck, Gladstone, and the Concert of Europe*. London. A perceptive comparison of Bismarck with Gladstone and the fullest account of the negotiations for the revival of the Three Emperors' League.

*Medlicott, W. N. 1965: *Bismarck and Modern Germany*. London. The finest short biography, especially sound on foreign policy.

Meyer, A.O. 1933: *Bismarcks Glaube*. Munich.
*Mosse, W. E. 1958: *The European Powers and the German Question, 1848–1871*. Cambridge. An important assessment of Bismarck's achievement with an excellent summary.
Nipperdey, T. 1983: *Deutsche Geschichte 1800–1866*. Munich. An outstanding recent synthesis.
*Pflanze, O. 1963: *Bismarck and the Development of Germany. The Period of Unification, 1815–1871*. Princeton. The leading comprehensive biography in English.
Pflanze, O. 1968: Another crisis among German historians? Böhme's *Deutschlandes Weg zur Grossmacht. Journal of Modern History*. 40.
*Pflanze, O. 1972: Towards a Psychoanalytic Interpretation of Bismarck. *American Historical Review*, 77.
Poschinger, H. von 1895–9: *Fürst Bismarck: neue Tischgespräche*, 2 vols, Stuttgart.
Pulzer, P. 1964: *The Rise of Political Anti-Semitism in Germany and Austria*. London.
Rich, N. 1965: *Friedrich von Holstein*, 2 vols. Cambridge. A full treatment, but uncritical of Bismarck.
Ritter, G. 1969–73: *The Sword and the Scepter: the Problem of Militarism in Germany*, vol. I. Coral Gables, Florida. An essential, conservative book.
Robinson, R. and Gallagher, J. 1961: *Africa and the Victorians*. London.
Rogge, H. 1957: *Holstein und Hohenlohe*. Stuttgart.
*Rosenberg, H. 1943: Political and social consequences of the Great Depression of 1873–96 in Central Europe. *Economic History Review*, 13. A seminal study.
Rosenberg, H. 1967: *Grosse Depression und Bismarckzeit*. Berlin. An expansion of his article.
Rothfels, H. 1970: *Bismarck. Vorträge und Abhandlungen*. Stuttgart.
Sempell, C. 1974: Bismarck's Childhood. *History of Childhood Quartery*, 2.
Sheehan, J. (ed.) 1976: *Imperial Germany*. New York. A collection of essays.
Silverman, D. P. 1972: *Reluctant Union: Alsace–Lorraine and Imperial Germany*. University Park, Pennsylvania.
Simpson, J. Y. 1929: *The Saburov Memoirs*. Cambridge. Important for the origins of the Three Emperors' League.
Smith, W. D. 1978: *The German Colonial Empire*. Chapel Hill, North Carolina. A competent survey with brief discussions of recent research.
Steefel, L. D. 1932: *The Schleswig–Holstein Question*. Cambridge, Mass. The standard account.
*Steefel, L. D. 1962: *Bismarck, the Hohenzollern Candidacy, and the Origins of the Franco-German War*. Cambridge, Mass. The best study in English.
Stern, F. 1977: *Gold and Iron: Bismarck, Bleichroeder, and the Building of the*

German Empire. London. An urbane treatment of an important theme, but it attributes too much influence to Bleichroeder.

*Stürmer, M. 1971: Bismarck in Perspective. *Central European History*, 4.

Stürmer, M. 1983: *Das Ruhelose Reich. Deutschland 1866–1918*. Berlin. A masterly synthesis.

Taylor, A. J. P. 1938: *Germany's First Bid for Colonies, 1884–1885*. London.

Taylor, A. J. P. 1954: *The Struggle for Mastery in Europe, 1848–1918*. Oxford.

*Taylor, A. J. P. 1955: *Bismarck: The Man and the Statesman*. London. A short biography written with a light touch but unreliable in detail and interpretation.

Townsend, M. E. 1930: *The Rise and Fall of Germany's Colonial Empire*. New York.

Waller, B. 1974: *Bismarck at the Crossroads*. London. Deals with the origins of the dual alliance.

*Waller, B. 1975: Hans-Ulrich Wehler on imperial Germany. *British Journal of International Studies*, 1.

Waller, B. 1976: Bismarck, the Dual Alliance and Economic Central Europe, 1877–1885. *Vierteljahrschrift für Sozial- und Wirtschaftsgeschichte*, 63.

Waller, B. 1982: Wirtschaft, Machtkampf und persönliche Rivalität in der Aussenpolitik Bismarcks vom Berliner Kongress bis zum Abschluss des Zweibunds. In Melville, R. and Schröder, H. J. (eds) *Der Berliner Kongress von 1878*. Wiesbaden.

Wehler, H. U. 1969: *Bismarck und der Imperialismus*. Cologne. Important and controversial.

*Wehler, H. U. 1970: Bismarck's Imperialism. *Past and Present*, 48. A summary of the German book.

*Wehler, H. U. 1984: *The German Empire, 1871–1918*. Leamington Spa. The translation of a remarkably successful and influential brief German textbook.

Wertheimer, E. von 1930: *Bismarck im politischen Kampf*. Berlin.

Index

Piedmont, *see* Italy
Pius IX (1792–1878), 57
Plamann School, 2
Poles, 27, 33–6, 56, 58, 69
power politics, *see* machtpolitik
primacy of foreign policy, 18, 65f
Prokesch-Osten, Anthony Count
  von (1795–1876), 21
Protestantism, 14, 57f, 78
Punch, 75

raison d'état, 8f
Ranke, Leopold von (1795–
  1886), 18, 66
realpolitik, 3, ch. 2 *passim*, 8f, 67, 76
Rechberg, John Count (1806–
  99), 21
reinsurance treaty (1887), 50, 81
religion: pantheism, 3; pietism,
  5–7; humility, 17
Robinson, R., and Gallagher, J., 71
Rochau, August von (1810–73), 9
Romania, 49, 81
romanticism, 13
Roon, Albrecht Count von
  (1803–79), 25
Rosenberg, Hans, 65
Rothfels, Hans, 32
Russia, 23f, 27, 42f, 46f, 49f, 71, 81f
Russo-Turkish war (1877–8), 43, 45

Saburov, Peter (1835–1918), 44
Schmitt, Carl, 77
social imperialism, 72f
social insurance, 60f, 65, 78

socialism, 40, 53–5, 58–62, 64,
  77–9
'splendid report' (26 April 1856), 23f
Stein, Karl vom und zu (1757–
  1831), 10

tariff, 59, 63–5, 67–70
Taylor, A.J.P., 19, 46, 71
Thadden, Marie von (1821–46), 5f
Thiers, Adolphe (1797–1877), 57
Three Emperors' League (1873,
  1881), 42, 49f, 70
Thun, Frederick Count von
  (1810–81), 21
Times, The, 25
Townsend, Mary, 69
Treitschke, Henry von (1834–
  96), 16, 55, 76
Triple Alliance (1882), 49f, 70
'two chancellors' war' (1878–80), 46

United Provincial Diet (1847–8), 10f

Virchow, Rudolf (1821–1902), 56

Waller, Bruce, 81
war-in-sight crisis (1875), 42f, 45
Weber, Max (1864–1920), 82
Wehler, Hans-Ulrich, 40, 63,
  71–4
William I (1797–1888), 17, 24–7,
  30, 60, 71, 75, 77
William II (1859–1941), 34, 75, 77f.

zollverein, 22, 26, 30, 67f